THE LOVE
AND
RESPECT

DEVOTIONAL

THE LOVE AND RESPECT

DEVOTIONAL

52 WEEKS TO
EXPERIENCE LOVE & RESPECT
IN YOUR MARRIAGE

DR. EMERSON EGGERICHS

W PUBLISHING GROUP

AN IMPRINT OF THOMAS NELSON

Published in Nashville, Tennessee, by W Publishing, an imprint of Thomas Nelson.

Published in association with the literary agency of Alive Communications, Inc. 7680 Goddard Street, Suite 200, Colorado Springs, CO 80920, www.alivecommunications.com.

Thomas Nelson, Inc. titles may be purchased in bulk for educational, business, fund-raising, or sales promotional use. For information, please e-mail SpecialMarkets@ThomasNelson.com.

Unless otherwise noted, Scripture quotations are taken from the New American Standard Bible®, © The Lockman Foundation 1960, 1962, 1963, 1968, 1971, 1972, 1973, 1975, 1977, 1995. Used by permission.

Scripture quotations marked BBE are from the Bible in Basic English.

Scripture quotations marked CEV are from the Contemporary English Version. © 1991 by the American Bible Society. Used by permission.

Scripture quotation marked GNT is from the Good News Translation® © 1992 American Bible Society. Used by permission. All rights reserved.

Scripture quotation marked GW is from God's Word®, © 1995 God's Word to the Nations. Used by permission of Baker Publishing Group.

Scripture quotations marked MSG are from *The Message* by Eugene H. Peterson. © 1993, 1994, 1995, 1996, 2000. Used by permission of NavPress Publishing Group. All rights reserved.

Scripture quotations marked NCV are from the New Century Version®. © 2005 by Thomas Nelson, Inc. Used by permission. All rights reserved.

Scripture quotations marked NIRV are from the Holy Bible, New International Reader's Version®. © 1995, 1996, 1998 by Biblica. www.biblica.com. All rights reserved.

Scripture quotations marked NIV are from the Holy Bible, New International Version®, NIV®. © 1973, 1978, 1984 by Biblica, Inc.™ Used by permission of Zondervan. All rights reserved worldwide. www .zondervan.com.

Scripture quotations marked NKJV are from the New King James Version®. © 1982 by Thomas Nelson, Inc. Used by permission. All rights reserved.

Scripture quotations marked NLT are from the Holy Bible, New Living Translation. © 1996, 2004. Used by permission of Tyndale House Publishers, Inc., Wheaton, Illinois 60189. All rights reserved.

Scripture quotation noted from the Phillips translation is from *J. B. Phillips: The New Testament in Modern English*, Revised Edition. © J. B. Phillips 1958, 1960, 1972. Used by permission of Macmillan Publishing Co., Inc.

ISBN 978-1-4003-3867-2 (RPK)

Library of Congress Control Number: 2011020229

Printed in the United States of America

23 24 25 26 27 LBC 5 4 3 2 1

For his tireless efforts in editing this devotional book,
I express my heartfelt thanks to Fritz Ridenour,
my friend and colleague,
and dedicate this book to his beloved wife, Jackie Ridenour.
On December 19, 2009, Jackie stepped ashore
and found it heaven,
breathed new air and found it celestial.

CONTENTS

CONTENTS

CONTENTS

The
Love & Respect
Video Devotional

The Love & Respect Video Devotional is made available free to you! Simply scan the below QR code and receive instant access to the *Love & Respect* video series. These inspirational videos complement the devotional you hold in your hands. Go deeper in applying the principles of love and respect in your marriage.

INTRODUCTION

Wanted: A Husband-Friendly Devotional Book

FIRST, A WORD TO THE HUSBANDS:

Gentlemen, what do I mean by a "husband-friendly devotional book"? I know too many men who feel that devotional books for couples are geared more toward women. That is why many of the illustrations and stories in these devotionals are geared toward men. I am not trying to give men a special pass or to be extra hard on women. No goodwilled man I know wants his wife treated unfairly. But at the same time, men don't want to be treated unfairly. A key reason for the success of *Love & Respect* is that it is fair and balanced. That is why many men get excited about feeling respected and then motivated about loving and treating their wives as equals. I am hoping wives will enjoy being challenged as equals with their husbands as they do these devotions together.

As Sarah and I travel the land giving Love & Respect conferences, we hear that wives want to have devotional times with their husbands, but their husbands shy away. Are most husbands avoiding devotional times with their wives because they are not good Christian men who believe the Scriptures and want to follow Christ? I don't believe that for a minute. Nonetheless, many couples have told me that the typical husband just doesn't find the typical devotional book for couples that interesting—or that friendly. After trying it a few times, he just sort of finds other things to do.

I think I know why. Most women experience an emotional and spiritual connection with their husbands when praying and reading Scripture together. The typical woman is energized by the typical couples' devotional because she is quite willing to share her feelings, her weaknesses, and her needs in order to feel oneness in her marriage. And she expects the same from her husband.

But if you are a typical husband, you are not that eager to be so transparent, and you don't see this as the primary purpose of a devotional book for couples. I know because I, too, do not get up in the morning with this kind of mind-set. Instead, I am thinking about fulfilling my responsibilities in my field of endeavor. Like most Christian men, I prefer to pray about what the Scripture is saying and how it applies to my tasks for the day and then commit this into God's hands.

But if I sense that Sarah might be using our prayer time to correct me or change my behavior to match her own Pink perceptions, I automatically start to feel resistant. Does this mean I am not interested in Sarah's needs or the needs of the rest of the family? Of course not, but my point is this: as I focus on Jesus during our prayer times, I am much more open to hearing His voice concerning something I might be doing to bug Sarah. I do want to be corrected, but not because Sarah has endeavored to change me during our devotional times. The changes come because God has spoken to my heart through His Word.

I am grateful that neither of us is trying to use devotional times to change the other. Sarah is committed to letting God be God in my life, and I am committed to letting God be God in her life. Our conscious attempt to approaching devotionals in this way is paying big dividends. We highly recommend it, and I also recommend "Options for Using This Book on Your Own Terms" (page xvii), which is full of ideas for using the fifty-two devotionals in this book to your best advantage as you seek to have God work in and through both of you.

AND NOW A WORD TO THE WIVES:

Ladies, may I be gently and lovingly honest with you? What I say may sound a bit stern, but please hear me out. If you have been to an L&R conference or have read the book, you are familiar with the principle of Pink and Blue. As a woman, you are approaching devotionals with a Pink view of life that is much different from your husband's Blue view, and this can lead to problems, as I have already mentioned.

In fact, it could well be that your big, strong husband lives in fear of your disapproval or criticism. With many couples the wife is often better versed in the Bible than her husband, and he probably doesn't feel he can "pray as well" to boot. In short, devotionals can make him feel vulnerable, like he is in a situation that will reveal his faults and flaws. Nobody—Blue or Pink—appreciates being in this position. It is contrary to human nature.

But even more threatening to a devotional's success is Pink's natural desire to want to "connect" with Blue while having devotions together. She pictures the devotional time as an opportunity to talk with her husband and share her feelings, in the hope that he will make changes that will make her feel more loved. I understand her womanly heart, but devotional time must not be seen as a vehicle for marital enrichment or therapy.

Am I saying that feeling emotionally connected to your husband during devotions is absolutely forbidden by God? Of course not, but let this be a by-product, not the goal. I was trying to make this very point when Sarah and I were having dinner with friends during the writing of this book. To help the wife process what I was trying to say, I asked her if I could use an outlandish example. She agreed, so I said, "What would you say if your husband wanted to have sex right after having devotions together?"

She frowned a little and said, "No way. Oh, I get it."

"Right," I replied. "This is about the two of you seeking Christ, not about connecting sexually or emotionally. That might happen after having devotions, but it is not your goal."

Feeling encouraged, I decided to make one more point. "On a similar note," I said, "let me try to convey what these big strong men feel about wives pushing them to read devotional books so they can 'connect.' What would you say if your husband said, 'We haven't read that diet book I bought you for a whole week'?"

She laughed out loud. "That's pathetic!"

"Yes, it is," I replied. "I'm not comparing devotionals to diet books, but I am comparing a woman's sensitivity to messages of disapproval with a man's. I don't know all the reasons why devotionals for couples have proven unsuccessful with so many men, but I believe the problem is rooted in a husband's fear of his wife's disapproval. He is not indifferent to connecting with Christ, but he is turned off by the thought that he must gratify his wife emotionally while having devotions together. Fearing that he will fail and be criticized, he stops showing much interest in devotional time together."

"I really get it," she said with a smile. "I see clearly what you are saying."

Ladies, perhaps some of you may think I'm making too much of all this, but please hear my heart as you would an older brother who loves you dearly. See this book as an opportunity to have fifty-two devotional times with your husband. Do not see any one devotional as something God will use to motivate him to better love you. I have seen too many men under that kind of pressure drift away, crushing the spirit of their wives who long to read scriptural thoughts and to pray with them. I have tried to make these devotionals as attractive to husbands as I can, while still appealing to wives. Please read "Options for Using This Book on Your Own Terms" (page xvii) for more on how Sarah and I have approached devotionals over the years, as well as many other ideas that can be of help. Use these devotionals with the goal of joining with your husband and believing that God is going to do something wonderful. Allow Him to work, and I guarantee He will!

AND FINALLY, A WORD TO BOTH OF YOU:

Obviously, if we hope to have husband-friendly devotional books, we have to do them differently. I am betting on my conviction that if we can create husband-friendly devotionals, the wives will happily take part. Remember, the key premise of Love & Respect is that if the wife respects her husband, he will in turn show her true love, and if the husband loves his wife, she will show him true respect. Yes, I am aware that this premise is not an absolute guarantee. There are always exceptions, role reversals, marriages with issues that need time to work out. Nonetheless, the Love & Respect premise has worked for thousands of couples. It has worked for Sarah and me. And it can work for you, too, if you hang in there, taking some time to look over the fifty-two devotionals in this book.

Some might ask: Why not more? Why not 365, like other couples' devotional books we've seen? Again, our research tells us that married couples don't want to deal with that much material, that often. So we consulted the survey results from the thousands of couples who have attended a Love & Respect conference, read the book, or watched the DVD. These couples have given us priceless feedback on what works for them and what challenges or hurdles still remain for them to overcome. We took the top concerns that surfaced in the surveys and developed fifty-two devotionals that discuss important Love & Respect scriptures and principles.

As I wrote the devotionals, I tried to keep them brief but still provide enough substance for busy people on the go. As the different topics took shape, they appeared to me like "mini-chapters," and so that is how they are organized: fifty-two brief chapters, each one a complete experience in reviewing each of the Love & Respect principles while you open yourselves to what God's Word has to say to each of you, then to both of you.

I am confident that if you spend devotional time together, the Lord will speak to you from His Word and draw near to you as you draw near to Him. Just always remember the chief (really, the only) ground rule: share what God is saying to your heart, not what you think He needs to say to your mate.

So let's get started. Put my husband-friendly devotionals to the test as you both seek to grow in Christ while reviewing, absorbing, and practicing key concepts from Love & Respect.

INTRODUCTION

≈

Note: All the devotionals in this book are based on Love &
Respect principles. If you have not been exposed to Love &
Respect ideas, you can get a brief overview in appendix B, "The
Three Cycles of Love & Respect" (page 273).

OPTIONS FOR USING THIS BOOK ON YOUR OWN TERMS

A s I worked with my creative team to develop something really different in devotionals for married couples, we came up with several options for how they can be used:

1. *Consider using these devotions separately, then coming together to compare notes.* Our research tells us that married couples don't always find it easy to "do devotions"—in fact, the opposite is the case. When we asked ministers at various churches how many couples were having devotionals together, the answer was "very few."

   One director of a marriage ministry at a megachurch told me: "The most successful couples' devotionals seem to be when the couple doesn't necessarily have to read the devotional at the same time. I know that sounds contrary to what we are trying to accomplish, but most of the couples I've counseled over the years have said: 'It feels really awkward to sit and read a devotional together, and after we read it, neither of us really know what to say.' I started suggesting they read it separately, then just talk about it throughout the week. This way it doesn't feel so forced."

Sarah and I would concur for a couple of reasons. First, there is no direct statement in Scripture commanding that married couples have devotions together (for more on this, see appendix C, "Devotions for Married Couples: Command or Option?" on page 281). Second, early in our marriage, Sarah and I did not have devotions together. We talked about it and decided to have them separately and then share with each other what we had learned. Sarah was relieved, saying it took a weight off her shoulders.

As for praying together, we would do that, but seldom did we pray for our marriage, because we felt it was just too easy to pray "at" one another and have one of us wind up feeling judged. Instead we would pray for our ministry and for people with needs, and as children arrived we prayed for them and about other family concerns.

Even today, we often read Scripture or other materials alone and then compare notes. And when we pray, we are always careful not to pray *at* one another. If you are recently married, or just starting to explore the concept of having devotions as a couple, am I suggesting you imitate our approach? Not necessarily, but I want you to know that it is an option. You and your spouse have the freedom to work out your own devotional life in a way that works best for you. I do believe, however, that because all of these devotionals are geared to review or reinforce Love & Respect principles, it is important to explore these principles together at some point, but only after each of you has considered individually what God has to teach you. The primary goal of your devotional time is to experience Christ's love. Your focus must be vertical, not horizontal.

2. *Use these devotionals at your own pace and convenience.* As you can see, these fifty-two short, undated devotional chapters are not organized for use on any kind of daily or weekly basis. Obviously, because there are fifty-two, the idea of doing one per week for a year comes to mind, but that is not required. It is up to the two of you to decide how often to go over a devotional, what time of day to do it, and the approach you want to take. Perhaps you will want to try the do-them-separately-then-compare-notes approach described previously. Or you may feel quite comfortable doing them together. There is no right way to use these devotionals. The best way is the way that works for you.

The following is one suggestion for how a one-chapter-per-week scenario might work. This plan is for a couple that is willing to try devotionals but may have reservations because of previous problems or even failures. You might call the following scenario "inching into the water a little at a time." Here are the suggested steps, which you can follow, adapt, or change, depending on what is comfortable for you.

- Choose to cover one chapter (devotional) a week.
- Start with chapter 1, which has been designed to launch the Love and Respect devotional. After that, you can use the other devotionals in any order you

wish—up to chapter 52, which is designed to close the book.

- Agree to read the devotional separately as your own schedules allow. Meditate on it and pray about it alone. Make notes you may want to share, but for an agreed-upon amount of time—even several days—work alone, allowing God to speak to you individually about your marriage.

   This is as far as some couples may want to go for at least a while. As spouses get used to the material, they may become ready to share with each other. Do not hurry this step. Just let it happen. Agree that you will make no judgments of one another if someone does not want to go on to what is suggested below.

- At some point during the week, come together to share what God has been telling you separately. Read the devotional together, and share any observations or questions you may have noted.

- Talk about the Insight (the boxed item that sums up the truth of the chapter). Pray, but only in a way that is comfortable. Use the Prayer suggestions or your own ideas. Be very aware of the danger of praying "at" each other, subtly (or not so subtly) asking God to change the other person according to your convictions.

- Consider the Action item at the very end of the chapter. Some of these are simple suggestions that individual spouses can apply as they see fit. Other Action items suggest talking together, and if you want to expand on this conversation, you can refer to the discussion questions in appendix A. This appendix includes several questions for each of the fifty-two chapters that can provide additional study and applications of the devotional truth each week.

This is just one plan for how to use the devotionals in this book. I believe there is enough material here for just about any couple, from those who are just getting started with having devotions together to seasoned couples who have had them for years.

Whatever approach you take, be determined not to get discouraged if you occasionally miss having devotions, for whatever reason. Life gets busy. You and your family may have hectic schedules. The important thing is to keep working at it. Let the Lord change you, but don't try to change each other. Be patient and trust Him. The goal is to have fifty-two devotionals with your spouse in which the two of you apply Love & Respect principles and focus on God together. I pray that these devotionals inspire, remind, and equip you to live out God's most important word to the church on marriage, as expressed in Ephesians 5:33. Oh the reward that will be yours!

AND THEY LIVED HAPPILY EVER AFTER . . . NOT NECESSARILY

PROVERBS 24:16:

For a righteous man falls seven times, and rises again.

O ne of our chief concerns at Love and Respect is not that people hear the message, important as that is, but that couples who attend a conference or read the book will go on to practice love and respect effectively in their daily lives. Of course, I realize each couple has this very same concern, and that's why my heart goes out to those I hear from who "get it" but who aren't able to "stay with it" consistently. They have learned that Love & Respect sounds simple, but it's not so easy to do. Maybe "not natural" is a better phrase. I understand. Sarah and I don't find it easy or natural either, and we have conducted Love & Respect conferences over two hundred times during the last ten years!

These are some of the many confessions I've heard from spouses who are struggling:

- "I'm desperately praying for the Holy Spirit to help me change and be a more respectful wife. It hasn't been easy though, and I fail much more often than not."
- "Love & Respect works great when we are practicing it, but we are not consistent. It's hard not to fall back into old patterns. I am so defensive it isn't funny."
- "I am continuously amazed at how quickly we can go for a spin on the Crazy Cycle. I want to cry thinking how my level of knowledge far outweighs my level of obedience."*

At this point you may be wondering: *Why is Emerson starting this book with such bad news from couples who fail? How can this help us?*

Hear me out. I am not trying to *discourage* you; I want to *encourage* you by saying right up front that Love & Respect is not a magic bullet. You will try it and find that you won't always practice it perfectly. To realize this truth and use it is a great source of strength and power. I love Proverbs 24:16 because it gives me such hope. Good people are not perfect, but God says: "A righteous man [or woman] falls seven times, and rises again." And how do you "rise again"? Here are three guidelines:

> **INSIGHT:** In marriage, it is never about not falling. It is always about getting back up.

1. *Never give up.* If you want to have a strong marriage, you need to accept temporary setbacks as part of the game. In

---

* If you are unfamiliar with the term *Crazy Cycle*, see appendix B, page 273.

baseball terms, keep stepping back up to the plate. According to the baseball statisticians, even Hall of Famers fail to get a hit seven out of ten times. And Babe Ruth, perhaps the greatest slugger of all time, struck out over thirteen hundred times, more than anyone of his day!

2. *Seek forgiveness from God and your spouse.* A wife writes: "I failed to communicate respect to my husband. I've asked the Lord to forgive me, and I am preparing an e-mail to ask my husband to forgive me as well." A husband reports: "I know now how I failed as a husband, friend, and lover, and I've asked God and my wife for forgiveness." Ephesians 4:32 says it all: "Be kind and compassionate to one another, forgiving each other, just as in Christ God forgave you" (NIV). Sarah and I often find ourselves turning to each other and saying, "I'm sorry—again."

3. *Ask God to take your hand.* Psalm 37:24 promises that though you stumble, you will not fall, for the Lord will uphold you with His hand. We need God's helping hand, and it's always there for us, if we ask Him humbly and confidently for guidance.

The storybook ending is always, "And they lived happily ever after." We know that's not really true because the slips, the bumps, and the falls do come in crazy ways. Life is not a matter of attaining some kind of marital nirvana. "Living happily ever after" means knowing how to deal with the imperfect parts of life—not accepting them with resignation but dealing with them through God's forgiveness and help and *always getting back up* when you fall. In a very real sense, the rest of this book is about just that, as you and your spouse will discover as you mine the riches of Love & Respect.

PRAYER: Thank the Lord for His forgiveness, His grace, and the righteousness that only He can bestow. Thank Him for His promise that though the righteous fall, they can rise again and continue to build a strong marriage with love and respect. Ask God to put it in your heart to refuse to let *defeat* defeat you.

ACTION: Make personalized copies of Proverbs 24:16 that say, "For a righteous spouse falls seven times, and rises again," and put them up on bathroom mirrors, inside cupboard doors, and in other places where you will see them every day. (For discussion questions, see page 215 in appendix A.)

PINK AND BLUE: NOT WRONG, JUST DIFFERENT!

GENESIS 5:2:

He created them male and female, and He blessed them.

O ne of the most powerful and eye-opening concepts in the Love & Respect approach to marriage is the difference between Pink and Blue. We aren't talking about how to decorate a nursery. We are simply pointing out how God made men and women as different as the colors pink and blue. I use the simple analogy that the woman looks at the world through Pink sunglasses that color all she sees. The man, however, looks at the world through Blue sunglasses that color all he sees. Men and women can look at precisely the same situation and see life very differently. Inevitably, their Pink and Blue lenses cause their interpretation of things to be at odds, in some cases more so than others.

Men and women not only see differently, but they also hear differently. To carry the Pink and Blue analogy a little further,

God created men with Blue hearing aids and women with Pink hearing aids. They may hear the same words but receive very different messages, as in the statement "I have nothing to wear!" She hears nothing *new*, while he hears nothing *clean*.

Because men and women figuratively wear sunglasses and hearing aids in different colors, they see, hear, and behave differently in countless ways: When she wants to talk face-to-face and he wants her to sit next to him and watch football, *this is a Pink and Blue difference.* When she wants their ten-year-old son to be more careful riding his bike and he wants his boy to ride that bike the way he himself did when he was ten, *this is a Pink and Blue difference.* When she wants to clean the kitchen, launder the sheets, and vacuum the carpet right away and he wants her to forgo these chores to play with him and the kids, *this is a Pink and Blue difference.*

INSIGHT: Pink must not claim that Blue is unloving because he thinks Blue. Blue must not claim that Pink is disrespectful because she thinks Pink.

Many couples arrive at our conferences suffering from "color blindness" regarding the profound impact the principle of Pink and Blue has on marriage, but when they leave, their color blindness is gone. They make observations like these:

- "I never saw that before. I thought we were the same."
- "Now I understand how men and women are 'wired' differently and why it takes a lot of work to learn about each other's needs."
- "I am able to view conflict totally differently now. Instead of seeing my husband as an egotistical maniac, I have some peace and confidence about who God made

me to be and who God made him to be, and I'm not feeling so frustrated about our differences."

Refusing to get frustrated is the key. Genesis 1:27 tells us that God made us in His image, and Genesis 5:2 adds that He *blessed* what He made. When differences arise (and they always will), remember this is part of God's plan. *Neither one of you is wrong, just different.* A major step toward a happy marriage is accepting differences and working them out with love and respect. Relax—and even rejoice. *Vive la différence!*

PRAYER: Thank the Lord that in the very beginning He created male and female—Blue and Pink. Ask Him for patience and ever-growing understanding of how men and women see and hear differently.

ACTION: When the Crazy Cycle threatens to spin over a Pink and Blue difference of opinion, try saying things like, "Here, put on my Pink sunglasses so you can see what I see," or "Here, try my Blue hearing aids so you can hear what I just heard." (For discussion questions, see page 216 in appendix A.)

CHAPTER 3

Do You Have a Goodwilled Marriage?

PROVERBS 11:27:

*He who seeks good finds goodwill, but evil comes to
him who searches for it (NIV).*

I am sometimes asked what I think is the most important
principle we teach. Pink and Blue (not wrong, just different)
comes to mind, but so does one simple word: *goodwill*. When
you and your spouse see each other as goodwilled, good things
are in store for your marriage.

When they first hear the word *goodwill*, people have questions: Just what is goodwill? How can I know I am showing
goodwill toward my spouse? How can I be sure my spouse has
goodwill toward me?

A simple definition of goodwill is "the intention to do good
toward another person." But the challenge often comes in when
one spouse does something to the other spouse that does not feel
"good," loving or respectful as the case may be. It is often just a

"little thing" but still enough to get the Crazy Cycle revving up. At moments like these, the "offendee" has to cut the "offender" some slack, as in giving him or her the "goodwill benefit of the doubt."

A number of verses confirm that goodwill is a biblical idea. See, for example, Proverbs 14:9, Philippians 1:15, and Ephesians 6:7. And Paul is surely talking about the concept of goodwill in 1 Corinthians 7:33–34 when he warns that husbands and wives can become so concerned about pleasing each other that they can be distracted from serving Christ as they should. Granted, husbands and wives don't always demonstrate that natural desire to please each other as well as they might, but their goodwill is real nonetheless.

That's why today's passage is so important. When there is conflict, disagreement, or a bump of some kind, don't automatically conclude that your partner has ill will toward you. If you look for evil (offense), you can find it every time. Do that and the Crazy Cycle will spin for sure.

What Proverbs 11:27 is saying to the married couple is this: look for the good in your spouse (even though it seems to be lacking). It is quite likely that you will see your spouse's goodwill coming right back at you. The truth is simple: *we will see what we look for.* No matter what happens, *always assume your partner has basic goodwill toward you.* How does that work in real married life? Here are some examples.

I know of one husband who made the decision always to assume his wife had goodwill. Not only did this simple commitment improve his attitude, but it also changed her entire attitude toward him! He writes: "I started giving her the benefit of the doubt . . . I didn't tell her she was disrespectful or anything . . . The results are stunning. She has been easier to live with. She doesn't nag me as much. She has shown increased interest in my hobbies. And she says I am like a new person." All this from simply giving her the benefit of the doubt! What does Proverbs 11:27 say? Look for good and you will find goodwill—sometimes in spades!

Or what about the wife who had to spend much of the summer apart from her husband because of their different career responsibilities? After several weeks she went to see him, meeting him at his office, where she knew he was under a lot of stress because of an important interview coming up. She hoped for at least a hug or a kiss but was greeted instead by a preoccupied husband who practically ignored her. Although she was hurt, she asked God to help her remember he was a goodwilled man who simply needed some time to prepare for an important interview.

Her prayers and patience paid off. Two hours later he "emerged a refreshed and lighter man, full of hugs and kisses for me." They had a wonderful time the rest of the eve-ning, as well as over the next several

> INSIGHT: Always assume your spouse has goodwill toward you, *no matter what.*

days. Before learning about goodwill and the Pink and Blue differences between men and women, she would have belittled her preoccupied husband in no uncertain terms. This time she turned to God for understanding and felt true peace because she was able to look at the situation from his male (Blue) point of view.

Does seeking good in your spouse when he or she has not shown much goodwill always work? No, not always, but remem-ber this simple but powerful principle: *assuming goodwill in your partner is always the best policy.* Keep on seeking the good; eventu-ally you will find it and goodwill as well.

PRAYER: Thank the Lord for the goodwill each of you has toward the other. Ask Him for strength to give each other the benefit of the doubt during moments when someone's goodwill seems to be lacking.

ACTION: During disagreements and conflicts, tell yourself, *my spouse has goodwill toward me—even though it doesn't feel that way right now.* (For discussion questions, see page 217 in appendix A.)

CHAPTER 4

GOD JOINED YOU TOGETHER, AND HE WILL KEEP YOU TOGETHER

MATTHEW 19:6:

So they are no longer two, but one flesh. What therefore God has joined together, let no man separate.

We are all familiar with the phrase "until death do you part" in the wedding vows. The Christian view is that marriage is for keeps, a value that is under constant attack in our present-day culture. Jesus' words are a powerful reminder that *God* has joined you together, not some human legal requirement. I hear from many couples who are very sure of this. Regardless of marital bumps, they say, "God brought us together, and that is all that matters," or "We *know* God brought us together," or (typical of our cyberspace times) "We met over the Net, and God brought us together in the most wonderful way."

Sincere believers agree with these enthusiastic testimonies and start out wanting to keep their vows, but for many, something goes awry on the road to wedded bliss. One spouse writes: "I believe in my heart that God brought us together, but we can't talk to each other at all without getting into a huge fight." And another says: "Because we felt so strongly that God led us together, we were so puzzled that after only one year we were so unhappy and having so much conflict."

Many couples may believe that matrimony is engineered by God, but this belief does not necessarily prevent acrimony. As Paul says, "Those who marry will face many troubles" (1 Corinthians 7:28 NIV). For precisely this reason, Sarah and I are committed to traveling the land—actually the world—spreading the word about the Love & Respect Connection, which can keep the marriage bond strong and, if necessary, heal hurts and pain from the past as one wife attests: "We made a promise to each other when we agreed to marry, that we would never divorce, *no matter what* . . . Love & Respect was the extra boost we needed to move beyond a negative stage, where we had gotten stuck. At last, we were able to give one another the benefit of the doubt and return love and respect to each other instead of suspicion and anger. I love where we are now in our journey together."

> INSIGHT: Because God joined you together, you can work out any problem, with love and respect.

Reread Matthew 19:6 carefully. You and your spouse are *one*, joined together by God, not to be separated by *anyone*. I used to think it took a third party to break up a marriage; now I realize that the greatest danger lies within. *Having challenges in your marriage does not mean you or God made a mistake; it simply means you must obey God's command to love and respect with renewed faith and commitment.* Like you, Sarah and I are committed to stay married until "death do us part," but if anything will kill a marriage it is anger, suspicion, and failing to give each other the benefit of the doubt. God brought us together and He will keep us together as we do our marriage as unto Him.

Of course, we know all this, don't we? I am simply reminding and urging you to *live* it every day, with love and respect.

PRAYER: Thank God for joining you together and for allowing you to trust Him to help you, whatever the issue. God is there for you and expects you to look to Him to keep you together as a team, so ask Him for His help in the smallest of concerns.

ACTION: During moments of irritation and disagreement, say words to this effect: "We know, in the big picture, that God joined us together. Let's look for His way past this. What are we doing that feels unloving or disrespectful?" (For discussion questions, see page 218 in appendix A.)

CHAPTER 5

THE 80:20 RATIO: THE SECRET TO APPRECIATING YOUR MARRIAGE

1 CORINTHIANS 7:28:

But those who marry will have trouble in this life (NCV).

In the book of Corinthians, Paul warns us of the responsibilities, involvements, and, yes, the troubles that come with marriage. When I quote 1 Corinthians 7:28 at our conferences, many in the audience chuckle, as if they understand perfectly what Paul is saying.

Something else that is tied to this idea of trouble in marriage is what I call "the 80:20 ratio." According to this concept, around 80 percent of the time, your marriage can be categorized as good or even great while around 20 percent of the time, you may have troubles of one kind or another. I arbitrarily chose 20 percent to make my point. For some couples it can be less or it can be more. It depends on many factors and can vary from week to week.

I cannot put a precise number on the amount of trouble you may have in your marriage, but what I do know is that God does not promise a fulfilling, trouble-free relationship 100 percent of the time. (I heard one man say he and his wife had twenty-eight happy years, then they "met and got married.") Disagreements and misunderstandings happen. Stress comes from without and within.

If we do not accept the inevitability of some trouble as part of God's design (that we will have moments when we feel unloved or disrespected), we may fall for the idea that a marriage should always be the perfect Hollywood romance. And then when troubles do come, we may conclude that we are not receiving what we deserve. If we expect 100 percent fulfillment, we will be ill prepared to deal with the moments when we feel unfulfilled or worse. We will grow discontented and resentful, and if we let these feelings dwell in our minds, it is not much of a jump to wondering if we made a mistake by marrying in the first place.

My point is simple: it is all too easy to focus on the 20 percent (the irritations and annoyances) and forget that 80 percent of the time things go quite well or even better than that. That pesky 20 percent of trouble turns out to be the leaven that leavens the whole lump (Galatians 5:9).

My solution is also simple. Do not live by the standards of Hollywood; trust what God says in His holy Word. Treasure your marriage like a bottle of the kind of expensive perfume women might like for Christmas, and don't let a few imperfections be like the dead flies that can give perfume a bad smell (Ecclesiastes 10:1). God has given you a meaningful lover-friend relationship; don't let the 20 percent—those times when one or both of you is tired, irritable, or just plain having a bad day (or moment) for whatever reason—sabotage your marriage.

My 80:20 ratio idea is an "aha" moment for a lot of people. When filling out a conference feedback form, they mention how enlightening the 80:20 ratio was and add comments like, "I realize I have a better marriage than I thought," or "Maybe my expectations of a 'perfect' marriage were unrealistic." Sarah agrees. She well recalls that early in our marriage she was concerned, not because we had major conflicts, but because the normal daily stuff was getting to her. To put it biblically, the little foxes were spoiling our marital vineyard just as it was trying to bloom (see Song of Solomon 2:15).

We continued to have our bumps, and Sarah continued to express her bewilderment about these tensions. Then one day I said to her: "Sarah, you want everything to be perfect. But Paradise has been lost. Sin is in the world. Eighty percent of what we experience can be wonderful; however, 20 percent will be troubling. If you don't grasp that, you will poison the 80 percent that's good."

> **INSIGHT:** Every marriage includes trouble some of the time. Do not let the 20 percent leaven all the rest.

Sarah says my little speech changed her entire view of marriage. The 80:20 ratio helped her realize there is no perfect relationship, and this came as a "huge freedom" for her, just as it did for me. We still have our 20 percent of troubles, but we just stop and remember that the 80 percent is really the big picture, and the big picture is what really counts!

PRAYER: Thank the Lord for all the trouble-free moments in which you and your spouse enjoy Him, each other, your family, your ministry, and life as a whole. Ask Him for the strength to accept your measure of trouble, and the wisdom to deal with the annoyances and irritations by loving and respecting each other with new commitment. (You may also want to pray about troubles at work, at church, or with the children, all of which can affect how you handle the 20 percent in your marriage.)

ACTION: Say in the face of a troubling moment: "Look, we will get through this brief storm. This is part of the 20 percent. Smooth sailing awaits us. For now, let's hang on to our hats." (For discussion questions, see page 219 in appendix A.)

CHAPTER 6

MISTAKES HAPPEN—AND THEN WHAT?

ECCLESIASTES 7:20:

There is no one on earth who does what is right all the time and never makes a mistake (GNT).

For Christmas, my daughter, Joy, gifted me with a whole season of *Gunsmoke* on DVDs. As a boy I enjoyed watching Matt Dillon, United States Marshall, and his friends Chester, Doc, and Kitty confront and defeat the bad guys in Dodge City, with every program also teaching a powerful moral principle. One evening I appreciated an episode entitled "Mistake." Matt Dillon misjudges a man, treats him unfairly, and challenges his honesty repeatedly. As facts surface, Matt realizes he is wrong, and he apologizes to the man but is still guilt-ridden concerning the whole sorry affair.

Chester tries to console Matt, saying, "It was just a mistake, and anybody can make a mistake."

"Yeah," Matt replies, "just a mistake, but it was *my* mistake, and it was a bad one. I can't wish myself out of it with a few words."

I understand how Matt felt, and maybe you do too. We feel horrible when we don't live up to our standards, which can happen often in marriage. To paraphrase King Solomon, author of Ecclesiastes, none of us does right all the time and everybody makes mistakes (see Ecclesiastes 7:20). I fail to love Sarah perfectly, she fails to respect me perfectly, and neither of us can "wish ourselves out of it."

What to do? Matt's good friend Doc offers him (and us) encouragement when he says, "Anybody can make a mistake, but it is a rare man who don't try to weasel out of it."

> INSIGHT: Mistakes can't be undone, but they can be forgiven.

Doc's grammar may be a bit lacking, but his wisdom is profound. All of us make mistakes, but instead of trying to find a sneaky "weasel way out," we can choose to do the loving or respectful thing. There are no more powerful words in marriage than "I was wrong; will you forgive me?" Those seven words aren't a magic wand that turns mistakes into pixie dust, but they go a long way toward helping us gain wisdom, empathy, and new resolve to improve our practice of love and respect.

PRAYER: Thank God for His forgiveness of your mistakes. In trying to be a loving man or respectful woman, we blow it. Owning up to mistakes is never easy, but it is always the way to move forward. Take good care not to accuse your spouse of mistakes as you pray. Also, pray about any forgiving to be done in the family, any forgiveness that needs to be asked. Children may need forgiveness (and what about Mom and Dad?).

ACTION: When mistakes happen (and they always will), deal with them by using powerful little phrases like "I'm sorry," "I blew it," "I apologize," and "please forgive me." (For discussion questions, see page 220 in appendix A.)

CHAPTER 7

QUESTION: WHAT IS LOVE? ANSWER: C-O-U-P-L-E

EPHESIANS 5:33:

But each one of you must love his wife as he loves himself (NCV).

I received an e-mail from Nathan, and he asked: "Husbands are to 'love' their wives. That's their special command. So what is love?" Excellent question. There are all kinds of answers, many of them rather flowery, syrupy, and some very romantic. I wrote back to Nathan with what I believe are practical, down-to-earth, biblical instructions on how a husband can spell *love* to his wife, providing six things described in chapters 8 through 14 of my book *Love & Respect*, by using the acronym C-O-U-P-L-E.

C-O-U-P-L-E

C: Closeness. You are seeking to be close—face-to-face—and not just when you want sex (Genesis 2:24). This is the idea behind cleaving.

O: Openness. You are trying to be more open with her,

sharing more of your heart and definitely closing off in
anger far less often (Colossians 3:19).

U: Understanding. You are pulling back from trying to "fix"
her and are listening more, trying to be considerate when
she's really upset (1 Peter 3:7).

P: Peacemaking. In order to resolve conflict and be united
as a team, you are trying to use the words of power:
"Honey, I'm sorry. Will you forgive me?"(Matthew 19:5).

L: Loyalty. You are exerting effort to assure her of your love
and your "until death do us part" commitment (Malachi
2:14).

E: Esteem. You are viewing her as your equal before God
and honoring and treasuring her as first in importance to
you (1 Peter 3:7).

The C-O-U-P-L-E acronym is the first half of the Energizing
Cycle, which teaches that "his love motivates her respect, her
respect motivates his love" (see appendix B, page 275). As Sarah
and I receive feedback, we are fairly sure people get it about
stopping the Crazy Cycle. But we wonder how well husbands
and wives are using the ideas in the Energizing Cycle. To have a
happy, biblically solid marriage, you and your spouse need to do
a lot more than just work on stopping the Crazy Cycle. And that
is where the Energizing Cycle comes in. When you keep the EC
humming, the CC stays in its cage and you function as the team
God wants you to be.

In this devotional I am suggesting that you and your mate
take a few moments to reflect on the love in your marriage.
What kinds of loving acts and words are happening? Right here,
one or both of you may conclude that I am putting all the pressure on the husband (these six things are, after all, what he is

supposed to be doing to connect with his wife). But that's not what I have in mind at all.

Using the C-O-U-P-L-E acronym, I want you to look for positives and plusses, not negatives and minuses. For many of us, it is all too easy to see the cup half empty instead of looking for the acts and words that make it half full, and often more. As a wife, guard against only seeing what your husband is overlooking; instead, appreciate his loving words and actions.

As a husband, guard against feeling that you can never be good enough; instead, receive encouragement from how you have been obeying God's command to act lovingly: "Each one of you also must love his wife as he loves himself" (Ephesians 5:33).

What is love? It is not a noun but a verb. It is something a husband does—in word and deed. One analogy is to picture the word *LOVE*, carved from a single block of beautiful oak or maple, bit by bit, day by day. Your marriage is like that block of wood. Love doesn't just happen; you have to work at it, and many husbands do. Remember, looking at the positive does not mean we are being naïve about the negative, but if any team looks only at its losses and never at its victories, it will grow discouraged. Winners need to celebrate their victories as an incentive to taste even more. Rejoice!

> **INSIGHT:** A wise husband recognizes ways God has helped him show love; a humble wife appreciates the loving things her husband is doing, and both celebrate.

PRAYER: Thank the Lord for the love that is evident in your marriage. Thank Him for where biblical love is being spelled out in your marriage: Closeness, Openness, Understanding, Peacemaking, Loyalty, and Esteem.

ACTION: Explore different ways to share love together. Need specifics? Choose from the sixty ideas located at the end of each chapter in the C-O-U-P-L-E section of *Love & Respect*. For example, just as this devotional encourages you to do, start by talking about the positive, loving things that are happening in your marriage, then go on from there. (For discussion questions, see page 221 in appendix A.)

CHAPTER 8

QUESTION: WHAT IS RESPECT? ANSWER: C-H-A-I-R-S

EPHESIANS 5:33:

And the wife must respect her husband (NIV).

The e-mail from Wendy stated: "I feel the biggest question or concern women have is, what is respect?" I wrote back to say I heartily agree; it is, in fact, the question wives ask me most. Not surprisingly, I answered it in much the same way I answered Nathan when he e-mailed to ask, what is love? (See chapter 7.) Respect, for a man, is not rocket science. I described six practical, biblical ways that a wife can express respect for her husband in chapters 15 through 21 of *Love & Respect*, using the acronym C-H-A-I-R-S.

C-H-A-I-R-S

C: Conquest. You are seeking to recognize and thank him for his desire to work and achieve for his family (Genesis 2:15).

H: Hierarchy. You are trying to thank him for his desire to be responsible in protecting and providing (Ephesians 5:23).

A: Authority. You are trying to pull back from subverting his leadership, albeit innocently, and are seeking ways to acknowledge his desire to lead and serve (Ephesians 5:22).

I: Insight. You are endeavoring to appreciate his desire to analyze and counsel by listening to the ideas and advice he offers (1 Timothy 2:14).

R: Relationship. You are valuing his desire for you to be his friend and stand shoulder to shoulder with him (Titus 2:4; Song of Solomon 5:1).

S: Sexuality. You are seeking to respond to him, appreciating his desire for sexual intimacy that only you can meet (Proverbs 5:19; 1 Corinthians 7:5).

The C-H-A-I-R-S acronym is the other half of the Energizing Cycle: her respect motivates his love. As I often share when speaking or writing, respect for the husband is a harder sell than love for the wife mainly because so many wives feel "he is failing to love me as he ought to, so he has to earn my respect." Of course, that is just the point. He doesn't have to earn her respect any more than she has to earn his love. Both are to be *unconditional*. God commands a wife to put on respect independent of who her husband is (1 Peter 3:1–2; Ephesians 5:33), just as God commands a husband to put on love regardless of his wife's lovability (Ephesians 5:25, 33; Hosea 3:1).

> **INSIGHT:** A wise wife recognizes ways God has helped her show respect; a humble husband appreciates the respectful things his wife is doing, and they both celebrate.

But what about Wendy's question: what, exactly, is respect? How does a wife show it? Note that all of the principles taught in C-H-A-I-R-S include the idea that the wife is to appreciate her husband's desire to succeed at work, protect and provide, serve and lead, analyze and counsel, enjoy her friendship, and engage in sexual lovemaking. The respectful wife seeks to honor her husband's desires, not because he is perfectly honoring her desires but because she intends to obey God's call to give him *unconditional* respect. She realizes this really isn't about her husband; it is God's command to her as a wife (Ephesians 5:33).

As you engage in this devotional together, take a few moments to reflect on the respect in your marriage. Using the C-H-A-I-R-S acronym, look for the positives and plusses, not the negatives and minuses. Husband, guard against making this an "I gotcha!" game by just looking for ways you aren't getting proper respect at all times. Instead, be thankful for your wife's respectful words and actions. And wife, don't feel defeated if showing respect may sometimes seem awkward. Like love, respect doesn't just happen. Like love, respect is something to be carved out a little bit each day as the wife obeys God's command "And the wife must respect her husband" (Ephesians 5:33).

According to Dale Carnegie, "Truly respecting others is the bedrock of motivation." When a wife truly respects a husband's desires as outlined in C-H-A-I-R-S, most likely he will be motivated to truly love her as outlined in C-O-U-P-L-E, and the Energizing Cycle will hum!

PRAYER: Thank the Lord for the respect that is present in your marriage. Ask Him for wisdom and guidance in appreciating and sharing the desires He built into men: to work and achieve, to protect and provide, to serve and to lead, to analyze and counsel, to enjoy shoulder-to-shoulder friendship, and to enjoy sexual intimacy.

ACTION: Use the suggestions at the end of the *Love & Respect* chapters on C-H-A-I-R-S, thirty-eight ideas in all, to explore and expand the concept of respect in your marriage. (For discussion questions, see page 222 in appendix A.)

CHAPTER 9

Newton's Law: The Crazy Cycle in Action

PROVERBS 26:21:

*Troublemakers start trouble, just as sparks and
fuel start a fire* (CEV).

As I sat there in the locker room steaming over a criticism by my military school swimming coach about not hustling, I looked up and saw a new cadet sitting on another bench, just staring at me.

"Quit staring at me," I said, "or I'll bust you in the mouth." I really wasn't interested in fighting, but it just came out. Obviously unruffled, he replied, "And I'll just bust you back."

Something about his nonchalant, totally fearless manner told me that this guy had been in a lot of fights before. I knew of cadets who got sent to military school to cure their street-fighting ways. The street-fighter's approach to life was an eye for an eye. You hit me, you'll get it back harder—sort of a living, snarling demonstration of Newton's law that for every action there is always an equal and opposite reaction. Discretion quickly over-came my burst of temper. To bust him in the mouth would have started something I was not ready to finish.

I threw no punch.

What does this little story of a locker room tiff and Newton's law have to do with marriage? If you have ever been on the Crazy Cycle, you know the answer: everything! To restate Newton's law in Love & Respect terms: for every disrespectful action by a wife, there can be an equal and opposite unloving reaction by her husband, and for every unloving action by a husband, there can be an equal and opposite disrespectful reaction by his wife. And the Crazy Cycle is on. Mix in their very different view-points—hers in Pink and his in Blue—and the Crazy Cycle can hum for quite a while.

Newton's law can be played out in marriage in endless ways. Sometimes it is all too easy to be unloving or disrespectful with-out meaning to, or realizing it—until it's too late. Here are two examples:

- A wife casually observes how well their friend Ben is doing in his business and is puzzled when, seemingly out of left field, her husband snaps, "Well, then maybe you should have married someone like Ben." She retreats, feeling hurt and unloved, to say the least. The Crazy Cycle has sprung to life.
- A husband innocently mentions to his prone-to-be-a-bit-heavy wife how well her sister is controlling her weight and is stunned to hear: "Yes, and my brother-in-law is getting quite a pooch, almost as bad as yours." The husband retreats into a stone wall of silence. He hasn't meant to be unloving—he was just making conversation—

and all he gets is disrespect. Chalk up another one for the Crazy Cycle.

What is going on in these two scenarios? Our key verse tells us that troublemakers start trouble, just as sparks and fuel start a fire (Proverbs 26:21). But neither spouse meant to be a troublemaker. She may realize that she might appear a bit disrespectful, but his unloving reaction is way over the top. And it may dawn on him that he may appear unloving, but she should know he didn't mean it. How come all the contempt in her voice? And that look on her face could freeze a water buffalo in its tracks.

Granted, in both situations we could claim that the offended spouse was too sensitive and responded immaturely. Nonetheless, accidental sparks (unwise remarks) ignite and fuel a fire, and *vrrooom* goes the Crazy Cycle. Newton's law is always at work. Your spouse is sensitive and vulnerable, and so are you.

> **INSIGHT:** One verbal punch usually begets a verbal counterpunch. Use words wisely.

Sometimes it is no accident. The Crazy Cycle can spin even more when anger goads you into *wanting* to make trouble. So when you hear what you think is a verbal punch and are tempted to throw a nasty response, step back. Was that really the Crazy Cycle starting to growl? I know whereof I speak. Sarah and I sometimes wind up squaring off, and then one of us has the good sense to say, "So do you want to get on the Crazy Cycle?"

That's not a bad way to defuse a situation, but an even better approach is to remember Newton's law and counter it with another law that will keep the Crazy Cycle in its cage: *thou shalt throw no punch!*

PRAYER: Ask the Lord for wisdom in how you talk to each other. Ask forgiveness for any verbal punches that may have been thrown, knowingly or unknowingly, and thank Him for your commitment as a couple to treat each other with love and respect.

ACTION: Write down some ways Newton's law can operate negatively because of what you do or say around your spouse. Then make it a point not to do or say these things. Why spark a fire? (For discussion questions, see page 223 in appendix A.)

CHAPTER 10

He Loves Us Because He Loves Us Because He Loves Us!

ISAIAH 62:5:

For as a young man takes a virgin for his wife, so will your maker be married to you: and as a husband has joy in his bride, so will the Lord your God be glad over you (BBE).

I t's no use. Love & Respect is a good theory. We both believe it, but it's so hard to make it work consistently. No matter how hard we try, we are always back on the Crazy Cycle."

I get this kind of e-mail comment almost every day. Sarah and I have felt like this many times ourselves over the past years. What is the best way to cope when discouragement strikes? Where should we turn?

Obviously, we should turn to God, but is that always reassuring? Maybe He is tired of our failures, our continual backsliding into Crazy Cycle craziness, or our unloving and disrespectful attitudes that pop up seemingly out of nowhere. For Sarah and me, it can happen right after we conduct a conference, sometimes in the airport or on the plane headed for home. There's nothing like fatigue to bring out our less-than-love-and-respect best—and then what?

What always works is to stop and realize how God really feels about us. *He delights in us as a husband delights in His bride.* This teaching is found in both the Old Testament and the New. Our key verse talks about how Israel, God's community of believers, is married to its Maker, and "as a husband has joy in his bride, so will the Lord your God be glad over you" (Isaiah 62:5). In despair in exile, the Israelites were told by God through Isaiah that whatever their failures, God had not given up on them.

The same kind of thinking is found in the New Testament when the church is likened to the bride of Christ. In fact, in Ephesians 5:22–33, the passage on which the Love & Respect Connection is based, Paul uses marriage as a picture of a much deeper truth. When a husband and wife are trying to live with love and respect for each other, they illustrate the relationship between Christ (the Bridegroom) and the church (His bride).

Do you grasp the fact that because you are part of God's bride (the church), God is your husband and He will delight in you forever? Do you *believe* this? Do you trust that God's vow to His people under the Old Covenant remains unchanging in the New Covenant that He made with us through Christ? He has chosen to delight in us and never, never forsake us!

So when you fail to love or respect completely, or maybe not at all, take heart. This isn't about us, but about Him. Mark it down: *He loves us because He loves us because He loves us!* We have nothing to do with it. Even when "we are faithless, He remains faithful, for He cannot deny Himself" (2 Timothy 2:13).

Yes, we can grieve the Holy Spirit (Ephesians 4:30), and He

may discipline us (Hebrews 12:5–6), but whatever happens, He accepts us (Romans 15:7) and He will *never* reject or discard us. Am I even remotely suggesting that it's okay to continue with sinful attitudes and habits and not work at love and respect because it is "too hard"? As Paul also said, "Certainly not!" (Romans 6:2 NKJV).

> **INSIGHT**: Your position in Christ is what counts, not your less-than-perfect performance.

What Sarah and I always do when guilty of un-Christlike behavior toward one another is ask forgiveness and determine to work even harder to reap the rewards of Love & Respect because it is "too good to disregard." We start again and seek to honor our Bridegroom because we know He loves us with an everlasting love. We never give up, because we know He will never give up on us!

PRAYER: Thank the Lord that He sees you as part of His bride in whom He takes eternal delight. Ask His forgiveness for any failures in your relationship and ask, too, for new strength and commitment to love and respect each other daily.

ACTION: Because God loves me because He loves me because He loves me, I will confess my failures, accept forgiveness, and seek to love or respect my spouse by _____.
(For discussion questions, see page 224 in appendix A.)

CHAPTER 11

HER PINK PLUS HIS BLUE EQUALS GOD'S PURPLE

EPHESIANS 5:31:

"For this reason a man will leave his father and mother and be united to his wife, and the two will become one flesh" (NIV).

As I have mentioned earlier, the analogy of Pink and Blue is one of the most remembered concepts we teach. For instance, before a conference ends I remind couples that Genesis 1:27 states, "So God created man in his own image, in the image of God he created him; male and female he created them" (NIV). I explain that in marriage, a Blue husband and a Pink wife each reflect the image of God, but I then take the analogy further and point out that when we blend Pink and Blue, we get Purple, the color of royalty, the color of God. In other words, *together* a wife and a husband reflect the royal image of God on earth. God is not Pink. God is not Blue. God is Purple. When two become one, they have the potential of displaying godlike qualities in their marriage.

But there is more. This blending of Pink and Blue into royal Purple is what Paul is talking about in Ephesians 5:31-32, when he speaks of a man leaving his parents to join with his wife to create the mystery of two becoming one flesh. And if you go back a few verses, you see he is ultimately referring to an even greater mystery: how the relationship between a believing husband and wife is the supreme illustration of the relationship between Christ (the Bridegroom) and the church (His bride). (See Ephesians 5:25-30.)

I am gratified that many married couples are blown away by this Pink and Blue imagery. One wife wrote to say, "The first thing that revolutionized my thinking and paradigm was the idea that the issues are not so much a Bart-and-Nancy thing as a male-female thing. That realization caused me to weep. It freed me so much to know that our differences of Pink and Blue will become Purple as Bart and I surrender and depend upon the Lord as we work through our issues." (Bingo! This lady gets it!)

I sometimes hear from spouses who wonder if two becoming one will rob them of their individual identities. My answer is that when two become one to mirror God's character, neither one loses individual identity. It is like overlaying individual pink and blue transparencies, which together project purple on the screen.

The metaphor of a team's oneness also captures the idea of all for one and one for all, as a husband and wife move forward united in their mission. In marriage he and she become a "we." The husband doesn't lose his masculinity, nor does the wife lose her femininity. But together they are more—much more!

At this point in a conference, the crowd often breaks into applause. The couples recognize that neither spouse loses any individuality as husband and wife hear a holy call being extended to them to become a team that reflects the Lord God. A husband

and wife who work as a team can make a life-changing impact on those around them, especially their children.

But the clincher to the entire Pink plus Blue equals Purple discussion is in Ephesians 5:33. The best and most practical way for two to become one is through the Love & Respect Connection. Oneness is undermined not through daily problems, but when he has an unloving attitude and she has a disrespectful attitude. Said in another way, if a husband and wife agreed on every decision, but she still felt unloved and he still felt disrespected, neither would feel one with the other.

INSIGHT: When Pink and Blue bond through love and respect, Purple happens!

But if a husband puts on love, especially during conflict, his wife will feel one with him. When a wife puts on respect during those moments of disagreement, the husband will feel one with his wife. A disagreement may not be solved, but oneness will be experienced. Two do, indeed, become one. Pink and Blue blend into Purple and God is glorified!

PRAYER: Thank God for His plan to blend and bond the two of you together. Thank Him that it is His will that you be one. Thank Him for the confidence He gives to empower you in your oneness. Ask Him for the wisdom, patience, and determination to make Purple the constant color of your marriage.

ACTION: When disagreements or other bumps come along, say, "One of us is Pink, one of us is Blue. How can we stay together in this and blend it into Purple?" (For discussion questions, see page 225 in appendix A.)

CHAPTER 12

IT'S ALL ABOUT PERSPECTIVE

PROVERBS 12:16:

*Fools have short fuses and explode all too quickly; the prudent
quietly shrug off insults* (MSG).

In an earlier devotional (chapter 5), I mentioned the 80:20 ratio and Paul's clear warning that in marriage we will have trouble (1 Corinthians 7:28). If we are to stop the Crazy Cycle, we must not let the 20 percent (the irritations and annoyances we cause one another) dominate our thinking and forget about the 80 percent (all the good things about our marriage). If we fall into that trap, the Crazy Cycle will start up in no time.

Point well taken. But there is another point to be made about 80:20. Not only is it good for stopping the Crazy Cycle, but it is good for keeping the Energizing Cycle going strong as we seek to motivate each other toward more love or respect. It's all about perspective. *To keep the EC humming, perspective is everything.*

I recall hearing a story years ago that vividly illustrates this truth. The widow of a farmer, recently remarried to another farmer, invited a group of farmers' wives for lunch. As the ladies were chatting, the woman's new husband came in from the barn-yard and tracked mud across the kitchen floor. All the women were incensed. One of them said, "If my husband muddied the floor like that, I'd kill him."

The newly married widow just smiled and said, "During my first marriage my husband often muddied the floor and I would have a fit. It caused some pretty tense times for us. After he was killed, his muddy boots sat empty on the porch. How I longed for him to walk through the kitchen in those muddy boots. I wept bitter tears because I had fixated on the mud on the boots instead of the man in the boots. Now that I have another hus-band in muddy boots, I really don't mind cleaning up the mud."

In marriage, irritations happen. We all suffer "muddy boots" annoyances we could explode about. The writer of Proverbs could have had the 80:20 ratio in mind when he bluntly called people with a short fuse "fools" and the patient ones "prudent." Marriage makes all of us sensitive to what we might think are "insults" at the time. But are they worth ruining the moment or the day or the week? Are they worth bringing the Energizing Cycle to a screeching halt while the Crazy Cycle revs its engines?

> **INSIGHT:** Focus on the positive in the midst of the negative, and the Energizing Cycle will keep right on humming.

Every day, usually several times, we have a choice: demand perfection from each other or accept reality. Perfection is impossible. The key to reducing anxiety and anger during imperfect moments is to roll with the punches. In other words, those who accept the 20 percent of trouble not only enjoy the 80 percent that is good but also find a way to deal with the troubling stuff that just doesn't seem to go away.

As I said earlier in chapter 5, the 80:20 ratio enabled Sarah and me to relax and enjoy the 80 percent a lot more. You may be wondering, *what does Emerson mean by the 20 percent?* Well, husbands won't want to talk and wives will want to talk too much. Husbands will appear insensitive and wives will appear overly sensitive. Wives will criticize and husbands will stonewall. Husbands will want sex on Tuesday night and wives will be too tired. The 20 percent is everywhere, sort of like the messes tracked in by muddy boots. So although Sarah and I still get upset on occasion, and although we still have less-than-perfect moments, we think we've learned at least one thing about marriage: perspective is everything!

PRAYER: Ask God for the wisdom not to draw huge conclusions from minor offenses. ("Love covers a multitude of sins" [1 Peter 4:8 NLT].) Commit yourselves before the Lord *not* to focus on the unloving or disrespectful moments. Instead, thank Him for all the Love & Respect blessings in your marriage. (Also, remember to thank Him for blessings on the parenting front and in the workplace. He is God of the 80:20 ratio in all circumstances!)

ACTION: Evaluate how well you are practicing the Energizing Cycle by writing down the skills or principles you are trying to use regularly as you practice C-O-U-P-L-E (for men) or C-H-A-I-R-S (for women). Are you keeping a proper perspective when "muddy boots" annoyances happen? Remember Proverbs 12:16, "The prudent quietly shrug off insults," and thus keep the Energizing Cycle humming. (For discussion questions, see page 226 in appendix A.)

CHAPTER 13

Those Who Pray Together Learn to Love & Respect Together

LUKE 18:1:

Then He spoke a parable to them, that men always ought to pray and not lose heart (NKJV).

In the introduction to this book, I made a big deal out of warning you and your spouse about praying "at" each other while having devotions. As a Blue I can attest this is not something I enjoy, and I think my Blue brethren would agree. In fact, as I researched this book, I learned that prayer is problematic for a lot of couples. Results from thousands of our research questionnaires reveal that 55 percent of married couples do not pray together. When I asked husbands and wives why, here's what I heard:

- "It just doesn't seem to work for my husband and me. It's awkward somehow. We try now and then, but then get discouraged and give up."

- "To be honest, I don't feel comfortable praying with my wife. I love her dearly, but I don't like being preached at during prayer together."

While the bad news is that 55 percent of the couples we surveyed are not praying together, the good news is that 45 percent are having prayer together as Love & Respect couples. But that's not all. Our research shows that couples who pray together are more apt to reap all kinds of benefits, including better and more frequent communication, going on "dates" more frequently, and having sex more frequently.

Do benefits like these prove that prayer is a magic bullet? Of course not. Anyone who has done much praying at all knows that you don't pray because of the "guaranteed benefits." Nonetheless, when you pray with faith, interesting things often do happen. One wife wrote to tell me that it "made her brain hurt" trying to explain why one rebellious child comes to the Lord and the other does not, why one person is cured of cancer and the other is not. But now she has a different approach. Her letter continues: "However, this year I have been blessed in many, many ways as I have turned my heart toward God. There are days filled with uncertainty, but when I look at the past year as a whole, there is an unmistakable guiding presence as I walk in obedience as a child of God."

> INSIGHT: At all times we ought to pray, not "for the benefits," but for the blessing of knowing we have obeyed His call to pray.

What I hear her saying is that prayer always "works" but not necessarily as she would like. She knows God always answers prayer: sometimes with a yes, sometimes with a no, and often with a "wait awhile." These three answers we all receive to our prayers coincide with what I teach: in marriage we are bound to have troubles at least 20 percent of the time or more (see chapter 5). If we pray "only for the benefits," when those 20 percent of troubles arrive, we may foolishly think that somehow God is letting us down and that being faithful in prayer (Romans 12:12) isn't worth it.

Over the years Sarah and I have sought to obey Jesus' command to pray, not for the "benefits" but simply because He calls us to pray. The deepest theological (and practical) reason for praying is to do so in obedience to Jesus' command to pray. Yes, we struggle (as do you) in learning to balance His promise to grant whatever we ask in His name (John 16:24) against the need to ask according to His will (I John 5:14). Nonetheless, we have seen Him work in remarkable ways after we pray. Yes, I know the skeptics can say that any answer we get is simply a coincidence, but we reply that when we pray, favorable coincidence after favorable coincidence happens, and when we do not pray, far fewer favorable coincidences happen.[1]

So as you continue the Love and Respect Devotional together, let me encourage you to keep praying and to not lose heart. As you pray together, you will truly learn to love and respect together. And it won't just be a coincidence!

PRAYER: Thank the Lord for the blessings that are always available in prayer. Ask Him for the wisdom to know the difference between "yes," "no," and "wait awhile." Praise Him for Himself, not for benefits you may think you want.

ACTION: If you are used to praying together, keep it up, with renewed commitment to obey Jesus' command. If praying together has been difficult, try making a concerted effort to pray together once a day for a week. Then discuss how it is going and what each of you can do to make the other feel more comfortable. (For discussion questions, see page 227 in appendix A.)

CHAPTER 14

WHO IS ON YOUR MENTAL COMMITTEE?

GALATIANS 1:10:

I'm not trying to win the approval of people, but of God. If pleasing people were my goal, I would not be Christ's servant (NLT).

She was late to her meeting, and she rushed to her car and backed out of the garage—without opening the door. Somehow, the door still worked, so she phoned her husband at the office to explain the huge dent, left a message, and dashed to her meeting. Later, when she pulled into the drive, she saw that he had gotten home first. Their two-stall garage had separate doors. In huge letters made with black electrical tape were the words HIS on the undamaged door and HERS on the damaged one!

Obviously, her husband wanted the world to know which door was which. He was concerned about what "they" would think. This apocryphal story makes a good point. We all have a "mental committee" called "they," who are the people whose opinions matter to us. Your mental committee includes all kinds of people: your spouse, boss, parents, close friends, and some not-so-close friends. In the case of the husband with a bashed-in garage door, "they" included the neighbors. He wanted all of them to know his driving skills were not in question.

It is important to note that sometimes we put people on our mental committee who should not be there because they negatively influence our lives in ways contrary to God's Word. The very human tendency to worry about what "they" might say is what Paul is talking about in Galatians 1:10. He knew that if he worried about gaining human approval, he could never please Christ. What he taught the Galatian believers, who were getting all kinds of negative pressure to please people who opposed the gospel, is still very relevant today for spouses trying to practice Love & Respect.

I hear the stories all the time. A wife knows she is to practice unconditional respect for her husband, and although it goes against the grain, she does her best because she wants to please God. But she also admires her feminist mother and her older sister, who are very cynical about men. When they mock and ridicule the idea of showing a husband unconditional respect, she puts the concept on the back burner, telling herself she will go easy with this radical idea so they won't disapprove of her. Pleasing big sis and Mom wins the day.

Similarly, a husband decides he wants to be a more sensitive, loving servant to his wife, who has two children in diapers. But his divorced father and unmarried brother, who work with him at the tool-and-die shop, scoff when he mentions he is helping with changing diapers and other chores. "Women's work is women's work," says Dad, and that settles it. The next time his wife calls and asks him to pick up some groceries on the way home, he whispers in his cell phone that he'll do it this time, but not to call him at work again. Pleasing Dad and his brother wins the day.

It is always good to take constant inventory of who is on your mental committee, especially the people who know you are trying to practice Love & Respect. Some of them are supportive, but some subtly, or not so subtly, question or even openly criticize. Family members often join the chorus, as do friends, fellow workers or club members, and even members of your Bible study group. Many couples tell me that when they decide to practice Love & Respect, they soon face decisions about whom they will please: the Lord (and each other) or someone else. It can get sticky.

INSIGHT: To act against the principles of love and respect is to displease Christ.

If you have people on your mental committee who are pressuring you to go against your better principles, remember that you put these folks on there. And you can take them off—quietly, lovingly, but firmly. They don't even have to know. But you will, and that will make all the difference.

PRAYER: Thank God that He anchors your mental committee through the Father, the Son, and the Holy Spirit. Ask Him for the courage to stand for unconditional love and respect for each other in the face of every kind of opposition—blatant or subtle. If you face no opposition, thank God for that too!

ACTION: Take inventory of your mental committee. Is there anyone you need to remove? Is there anyone you need to add? (For discussion questions, see page 229 in appendix A.)

CHAPTER 15

TO TELL THE TRUTH . . . IS NOT ALWAYS EASY

EPHESIANS 4:25:

So stop telling lies. Let us tell our neighbors the truth, for we are all parts of the same body (NLT).

C an practicing love and respect lead to acting "too nice" even when you feel hurt or irritated by something your spouse does? According to the e-mails I receive, it is no small problem. Husbands and wives seem equally affected by the idea that living the Love & Respect way means you must keep the peace by remaining silent to avoid conflict.

They have mistakenly concluded that somehow it is best to remain quiet when feeling unloved or disrespected. They reason that if they were "really spiritual," they would not have negative feelings, so when irritations happen they suppress those feelings. We tell them that while they mean well with this approach, it is not healthy to be too accommodating on matters that matter. In fact, avoiding the Real Issue—feeling unloved or disrespected—can actually be unloving or disrespectful in the long run, and the Crazy Cycle will hum.

It may be tempting to avoid potential conflict by saying nothing, but Scripture does not advise this approach. While there is "a time to be silent," there is also "a time to speak" (Ecclesiastes 3:7 NIV).

And as difficult as it may be during those "times to speak," we should speak the truth. Your spouse deserves the truth from you, even if you are prone to "put yourself in neutral" and let others push you around. Take small but steady steps to learn to decode your negative feelings, and then be honest with your mate. The key, of course, is to tell the truth—gently.

Unfortunately, it is all too easy to "be honest" in a way that triggers an argument, which escalates into a fight. Then it's natural enough to conclude that your spouse did not want to hear what you had to say. Not so. The *way* in which we speak incites the conflict, not the content.

So we need to change our speaking ways, as did one wife who needed to speak up truthfully in order to clarify what her husband was feeling, as well as to make clear how she was feeling. She explained, "My biggest struggle is with assuming that he is thinking bad things about me, and with reading bad intentions into his innocent statements. Gradually, I'm learning to communicate my fears to him, to react in a more respectful manner when I'm feeling hurt, and to accept the love that he shows me in so many ways."

INSIGHT: Suppressing negative feelings is not loving, respectful, or very wise. Speak up—tactfully.

This lady gets it. Today's key verse is positioned within a

larger context that has much to say about Christian relationships, including marriage. Writing to the Ephesian church, Paul says, "throw off your old sinful nature and your former way of life . . . Instead, let the Spirit renew your thoughts and attitudes" (Ephesians 4:22–23 NLT). Then in his first specific suggestion for how to do this, he says, "So stop telling lies. Let us tell our neighbors the truth, for we are all parts of the same body" (Ephesians 4:25).[1]

When Paul says "we are all parts of the same body," he speaks of the church body, which certainly includes all married believers. Then, too, who is a closer "neighbor" than your spouse?

Your spouse deserves the truth from you. Do your best to tell it with love and respect.

PRAYER: Ask the Lord to empower you to speak the truth to each other humbly and gently when feeling unloved or disrespected. Ask Him to help you understand that it is futile to let these things go by because a "good spouse shouldn't feel this way." Thank Him in advance for helping you have a marriage where there is ever-growing love and respect.

ACTION: One couple I know puts little signs around their home that say, "Talk to me like you LOVE me," and "Talk to me like you RESPECT me." What better way to make it easier to tell each other the truth? (For discussion questions, see page 230 in appendix A.)

CHAPTER 16

FEELINGS AREN'T FACTS— ALWAYS SORT IT OUT

PROVERBS 16:25:

*Some people think they are doing right, but in the
end it leads to death* (NCV).

We have seen what *suppressing* feelings can do to put a
marriage on the Crazy Cycle (see chapter 15). What
about *expressing* feelings that may be seriously mis-
taken? As you seek to practice Love & Respect, it seems all too
easy to get into a simple disagreement, maybe an argument. At
moments like these it is easy for Pink to feel unloved and Blue
to feel disrespected.

For example, as a disagreement begins to heat up, Blue may
suddenly grow aloof and distant, making Pink feel like a door-
mat. She may feel she is absolutely right in thinking her husband
can act like the most unloving man on the planet.

Or perhaps it is Blue who feels attacked. All he is trying to
do is express his opinion, yet Pink suddenly seems to be scolding

him, not letting him get a word in edgewise. He may think he has every reason, at least at the moment, to believe he is married to a close cousin of the Wicked Witch of the West.

But do these exaggerated feelings that can flash into our minds necessarily fit the facts? A husband who seems cold and aloof may simply be pulling back because he feels outflanked by his verbal wife, and he just needs to calm down. It may feel unloving to his wife, but her feelings can be wrong. A wife who comes off as demanding or scolding may simply be feeling fearful and insecure, and what she really wants is reassurance that she is loved. It may feel disrespectful to her husband, but his feelings can be wrong.

Some of the examples I use may sound extreme, like people really riding the Crazy Cycle, but wherever you are on board "facts versus feelings," the point is well taken: it is all too easy to say or do things that hurt and lead to bad feelings of one degree or another. And it is also easy to become convinced that your feelings are right, even to the point of thinking it's the voice of the Holy Spirit telling you how your spouse is failing to love or respect you!

But feelings aren't facts. As Proverbs 16:25 teaches, what "seems right" can be far from the facts. In fact, it can be so far off that it can "lead to death." Scholars point out that the Hebrew word for "death" can also be figuratively translated as "ruin." In that case "what seems right" can ruin the conversation, ruin the entire evening, ruin any hope for sexual intimacy, ruin the relationship, and, eventually, ruin the marriage.[1]

In Matthew 18, Jesus demonstrates how important it is to confirm the facts when he reaches back into Jewish law to teach His disciples not to allow emotions to win the day when confronting people in sin (see Deuteronomy 19:15). Jesus was speaking of applying church discipline, but I have used His principle to counsel many married couples who immediately recognize its sound application to them: *we must talk about facts, not just feelings.* When feelings cause heated accusations to rise on the tip of your tongue, it is time to step back and say, "I am feeling unloved (or disrespected) because of how I am reading what you say and do. We are about to spin on the Crazy Cycle. Let's talk about my feelings and try to get to the facts."

INSIGHT: What "seems right" can ruin everything. Get the facts!

Sarah and I use this approach, rather than trusting feelings that may *seem right* but can eventually ruin our relationship. Sometimes, when things get emotional and one (or both) of us just knows "I am right," it is hard to calm down and focus on the facts, but it is always worth it. We hope you do the same—always out of love and respect!

PRAYER: Acknowledge that feelings of being unloved or disrespected can be accurate, though not always. Thank God for the biblical principle that every fact must be confirmed. Confess that feelings do not always equal His voice, and ask for wisdom in sorting out feelings from facts, while giving each other love and respect. (You may also want to pray about situations at work, or possibly at church, where strong feelings may be confusing the facts.)

ACTION: Always keep in mind that Pink and Blue wear different sunglasses and usually see the facts differently. When feelings are growing strong, allow each person to describe the facts while the other listens carefully to what is said. Then work toward a solution. (For discussion questions, see page 231 in appendix A.)

CHAPTER 17

WHAT IS REALLY GOING ON HERE?

PROVERBS 15:13:

When the heart is sad, the spirit is broken.

Early in our marriage I was working as a counselor, driving to seminary classes seventy miles one way, conducting small groups, living on a fixed budget, and trying to be a good husband and father. It was an overwhelming schedule and I had little time to spend with Sarah. There were moments when Sarah, too, was feeling overwhelmed and, being a typical Pinkie, she wanted to talk.

"You never spend time with me and are always busy," she would say, and as she now recalls, every so often she could see my spirit deflate because she pushed me too far. In frustration I would hold up my hand and say, "That's enough!" Then I would stonewall her by refusing to talk at all. What neither of us understood at the time was that her disrespect had shut me down. I felt like she was telling me that I was an inadequate man.

Years later I discovered that sometimes what seems to be the issue isn't the real issue. As Sarah and I look back on those early years, we see that the apparent issue—that we weren't spending enough meaningful time together—was an important one, but the Real Issue that shut me down and caused me to stonewall her was that I felt disrespected.

At other times, I deflated Sarah. For example, I recall trying to explain away why I was not listening to her when she was sharing her heart. Not only did I fail to engage and empathize, but I ended up making a lame excuse, such as, "I got distracted by a thought I just had." That would send her into utter frustration, and her spirit would sink. The issue—that I wasn't listening—became another deeper issue: she felt unloved, like she did not matter to me. Though I did not break her spirit, she felt that I was pulling away from her, disconnecting from her emotionally. Even though I didn't understand the Real Issue, I could sense that if I continually treated Sarah in ways that felt unloving to her, I could break her heart.

The key verse for today warns us that "when the heart is sad, the spirit is broken" (Proverbs 15:13). That is why, when your spouse's countenance, or words, seem to be describing something more serious than the topic at hand seems to warrant, it is good to pay close attention and look deeper. In an Old Testament scene, Jacob was puzzled, then provoked, when his wife Rachel got upset and blatantly blurted, "Give me children or I die!"

Angrily, Jacob shot back, "Am I in the place of God, who has kept you from having children?" Rachel wasn't really threatening suicide. Jealous of her sister because she could not bear Jacob a child, Rachel simply needed reassurance that they could trust God together concerning children. The real issue was that Rachel needed love and understanding, and Jacob missed it (see Genesis 30:1–2).

So often, when one spouse's heart is sad, frustrated, or angry, the apparent issue is not the issue at all. For many years now, Sarah and I have both looked for the deeper issue of feeling unloved or disrespected and have been able to defuse emotions threatening to get out of control. It is amazing how many conflicts you can circumvent when you discern what is really going on.

INSIGHT: Often the apparent issue isn't the real issue; the real issue is always a matter of love or respect.

I know you can do the same because I continually hear the testimony of couples who are joining us in detecting when an issue is getting out of hand. As one wife said, "Tom and I were disagreeing the other night and he said, 'Now, let's not get on the Crazy Cycle.' We were able to resolve our issue (which almost became a Love & Respect issue!) and feel closer as a result."

And to that I say, "Amen!"

PRAYER: Thank the Lord for the wisdom in Proverbs 15:13, a wisdom that enables you to discern that sometimes when a heart is sad, something deeper is going on in that person's spirit. Ask for guidance in always looking for the real issue—are you giving each other love and respect? (You may want to add some time for prayer for issues involving your children right now. Ask for the wisdom to discern the Real Issue—somebody may be feeling unloved or disrespected.)

ACTION: When you have an issue that is getting out of hand, one of you can say, "I feel the Crazy Cycle coming on. Let's discuss this quietly and not let it turn into one of us feeling unloved or disrespected." (For discussion questions, see page 232 in appendix A.)

CHAPTER 18

JOHN WOODEN:
A LOVE & RESPECT
LEGACY FOR THE AGES

PROVERBS 3:35:

*The wise will have glory for their heritage, but shame will
be the reward of the foolish* (BBE).

While I was working on this book, the news came in on TV, radio, and the Internet: John Wooden, the legendary UCLA basketball coach, had transitioned from this planet to heaven just four months short of his one hundredth birthday.

His athletic achievements were incredible. Born in 1910, just nineteen years after the game of basketball was invented, Wooden led his high school basketball team to the Indiana state championship, then went on to help take the Purdue Boilermakers to the NCAA title and be named College Player of the Year. But his real fame was to come as coach of the UCLA Bruins, from 1948 to 1975; his teams had four perfect 30–0 seasons, eighty-eight con-secutive victories, thirty-eight straight NCAA tournament wins, twenty PAC-10 championships, and an unprecedented, never equaled achievement of ten NCAA national championships.[1]

As the reports and accolades poured in, the word *legacy* (or *heritage*) came quickly to mind. Known fondly as Coach, John Wooden will be remembered for teaching his players first to be men of honor with solid values. His Pyramid of Success adorns countless walls and is still taught far and wide. His famed say-ings, known as *Woodenisms*, are quoted continually. Here are just a few of the dozens of sayings he used to inspire and instruct his teams:

- If you don't have time to do it right, when will you have time to do it over?
- Talent is God-given. Be humble. Fame is man-given. Be grateful. Conceit is self-given. Be careful.
- Failure is not fatal, but failure to change might be.[2]

John Wooden became a Christian as a junior in high school, and he let his faith in Christ drive all he did as a player, coach, teacher, and husband. In an inter-view granted near the end of his life, Wooden stated: "There is only one kind of life that truly wins, and that is the one who places faith in the hands of the Savior. Until that is done, we are on an aimless course that runs in circles and goes nowhere."[3]

> **INSIGHT:** To build a lasting legacy, use proven wisdom that you glean from the Lord.

What also grabbed my attention about John Wooden is that

he excelled in the field of marriage, perhaps more than in anything else. He married his high school sweetheart, Nell, just after graduating from Purdue in 1932. His romance with Nell lasted fifty-three years, and after she succumbed to cancer on March 21, 1985, it continued as he wrote her a love letter on the twenty-first of every month for the next twenty-five years. In those letters he expressed his love, confessed how much he missed her, and shared news about their children, grandchildren, and great-grandchildren.[4]

John's marriage to Nell ended well before the birth of the Love & Respect Connection, but it is clear that they practiced love and respect instinctively. Comparing his long and happy marriage to his walk with the Lord, he said, "Both require hard work, but the benefits are worth it." Wooden spoke of how his marriage to Nell had taught him the importance of finding peace within yourself so that you can overlook the flaws in others, and learn how to work through misunderstandings.[5]

As I thought about John Wooden's life, I realized what it was that made him such an outstanding human being: *he was a man who lived by biblical principles.* How he lived and what he taught enabled him to leave behind a legacy built on his commitment to Jesus Christ. Truly, as our proverb for today says, "The wise will have glory for their heritage." The glory spoken of here is that which ultimately glorifies the Lord, and this was clearly John Wooden's life goal.

Few of us could ever equal John Wooden's achievements, but we can all emulate him by building a lasting legacy to bless those who come after us. Here is one more Woodenism that you can practice daily with your spouse and family:

- Consider the rights of others before your own feelings, and the feelings of others before your own rights.[6]

There is no more practical way than this to put uncondi-tional love and respect into action! These are words you can use every day to build a legacy that will never fade. As Coach put it, "Material possessions, winning scores, and great reputations are meaningless in the eyes of the Lord, because He knows what we really are and that is all that matters."[7]

PRAYER: Thank God for the life of a man like John Wooden and ask Him for the commitment to practice the kind of wisdom Wooden lived as a coach, teacher, and spouse. Ask Him to help you learn how to work through mistakes and misunderstandings, small or not so small. Ask Him to help you both work just a bit harder to love and respect, always remembering that ongoing success in marriage takes character—the kind that comes from the Lord.

ACTION: Take a few minutes to write down the legacy you would like to leave behind. When you are gone, how do you want people to describe you? (For discussion questions, see page 233 in appendix A.)

CHAPTER 19

FORGET THE NEGATIVE SNAPSHOTS—ENJOY THE POSITIVE MOVIE

MATTHEW 7:1–3:

Stop judging others, and you will not be judged. For others will treat you as you treat them . . . And why worry about a speck in your friend's eye when you have a log in your own? (NLT)

A word picture I sometimes use is my "snapshot" versus "movie" approach to marriage. What I mean is this: there are moments when your spouse will be unloving or disrespectful. I call these moments *snapshots*. They happen, but they are not the whole picture or the *movie* of your spouse's life, most of which is positive.

It's the 80:20 ratio all over again (see chapter 5). The 80 percent is your spouse's positive behavior—the movie, if you please, of who your spouse really is: a person of goodwill who never means to harm you. The 20 percent are those occasional negative comments or actions (snapshots) that can make you think your spouse does not have goodwill toward you. In fact, look at these snapshots long enough and you will start judging your spouse, impugning motives, and assassinating character. The Crazy Cycle is ready to roll!

It's easy to do. Any couple can snap a few local snapshots of each other at less-than-good moments, then replay them in the album of their minds and proceed to make global judgments that are not really accurate. For example:

LOCAL SNAPSHOT: "See, right here, he was not listening to me as we ate dinner." Global judgment: "He is so uncaring and unloving!"

LOCAL SNAPSHOT: "Look! She is overspending her clothing budget again." Global judgment: "She is so uncontrolled and disrespectful."

LOCAL SNAPSHOT: "See how angry he got over nothing out in the kitchen just before dinner." Global judgment: "He is so mean and unloving."

LOCAL SNAPSHOT: "Here's one in the bedroom, when she said no to sex on Tuesday night." Global judgment: "She is so frigid and dishonoring."

The big danger in playing the snapshot game is that the snapshot may be true, but the judgment is exaggerated and false. It is so easy to draw wrong conclusions about a spouse's character and motives due to an occasional flare-up or silly comment. In biblical terms, making that kind of judgment is equal to spotting the speck in your spouse's eye and missing the log in your own. Jesus described this problem in Matthew 7, when He taught us to stop judging others (and that certainly includes a spouse).

Truth be told, all of us have specks in our eyes. A wife can see her husband as unloving, but is she always unconditionally respectful? A husband notes when his wife is disrespectful, but is he always unconditionally loving? Why get so self-righteous and indignant? If you intend to hold up a negative snapshot of your spouse, be aware you will have to acknowledge plenty of unfavorable snapshots of yourself!

Judging others is a no-win process, but I constantly receive e-mails from people who typically list from three to ten negative snapshots of what their spouses are doing. They give this report so I will "understand, empathize, and offer advice." Some are simply building a case against their spouse; most want to do what God wants, but they are baffled about how to improve their marriage.

To help them make an adjustment, I give this assignment: "Make a list of five to ten positive things about your spouse. Then send the list to me." That exercise frequently changes the person's perception as he or she experiences some Kodak moments!

> **INSIGHT:** Saving lots of negative snapshots can spoil precious memories. Concentrate on the ongoing movie.

Those positive qualities become a bigger picture, a movie that is attractive and compelling. Many women have said, "I fell in love with my husband all over again." The point to this exercise (and this devotional) is simple: we all take a snapshot now and then, but the long-running movie is what counts!

PRAYER: Give thanks that both of you are goodwilled people whose lives are like positive movies that are true pictures of who you are. Ask the Lord for the wisdom not to let occasional negative snapshots cause you to judge each other unfairly.

ACTION: When the same negative snapshot keeps popping up, sit down with your spouse and share how and why you feel unloved or disrespected. Do not attack motives or character; keep looking for the bigger positive picture. (For discussion questions, see page 234 in appendix A.)

CHAPTER 20

SEX AND AFFECTION: A TWO-WAY STREET

1 CORINTHIANS 7:3:

*The husband should fulfill his marital duty to his wife,
and likewise the wife to her husband (NIV).*

Feeling that his sexual appetites are waning, the husband asks his doctor if something might be wrong. The doc says, "Walk five miles a day for the next three weeks and call me and tell me how you're doing." Three weeks later the husband calls, and the doc asks, "So . . . how is the sex?" The husband replies, "How am I supposed to know? I haven't seen my wife in three weeks, and I'm 105 miles from home."

"So . . . how is the sex?" If there was ever an issue that can quickly become a love and respect issue, it is this. Fortunately, Paul leaves some good advice to help couples keep sex in a positive perspective, providing they are willing to work together to benefit one another. He says, "The husband should fulfill his marital duty to his wife, and likewise the wife to her husband"

(1 Corinthians 7:3). That's what it says in the *New International Version*, and almost the same wording is in the *New American Standard Bible*. At first glance it sounds as though Paul thinks sex is an obligation, to be done begrudgingly if necessary. And, true enough, the Greek word here for "duty" means we are to give the other person what is due, as if we have a debt to pay.

There is, however, another way to translate this Greek word that throws light on the problem: "Husbands and wives should be fair with each other about having sex" (CEV). And in the Phillips translation we read: "The husband should give to his wife what is due to her as his wife, and the wife should be as fair to her husband." When fair play precedes foreplay, husband and wife are tuned in on satisfying each other sexually *and affectionately*: "Let the husband render to his wife the affection due her, and likewise also the wife to her husband" (NKJV). Each is focusing on giving, not receiving, and that makes sex an entirely different ball game from the one too many couples play, which often leads to making it an issue that obscures the Real Issue: feeling unloved or disrespected.

> **INSIGHT:** Fair play should always precede foreplay.

Over the years I have received literally thousands of e-mails from spouses who struggle with the issue of being fair with each other about sex. Typically, the husband's primary need is for sexual release, which only his wife can meet, and the wife's primary need is for affection and a feeling of emotional connectedness. (There are exceptions to these general leanings. For example, I get e-mails from a substantial number of women who say they are the ones who need sex more often.)

Not surprisingly, if one spouse's need is not met, he or she will not be inclined to want to focus on the need of the other. And so it seems to be a standoff. The wife can say, "Lovingly meet my needs for affection and connection and I'll respond sexually." The husband can answer, "Respectfully meet my sexual need, since you alone can meet that need, and I'll respond to your emotional needs." This is the kind of quid pro quo dance many couples do, but it is not what Paul means in 1 Corinthians 7 when he talks about being fair to one another. Obviously, Paul is not saying one spouse can mandate "sex for affection" or that the other can mandate "affection for sex."

Sex and affection are the best proving grounds to help you and your spouse grow in love and respect for each other—physically, emotionally, and intimately. Look at the sexual aspect of your relationship as a compliment to how important you are in your spouse's life. You are the only person who can meet this need in your spouse!

Chapter 31 will have more to say about the sex–affection issue and how it relates to "mutual submission." For now, however, focus on the fact that the two of you have legitimate Pink and Blue needs that must be met fairly, lovingly, respectfully. Neither is wrong, just different.

If one partner is not being as responsive as the other might like, Christ is calling someone to make the first move. (Maybe He is calling *both* of you!) As two mature people, can you talk it through and work it out? There is no need to go three weeks without sex or affection and wind up "105 miles from home."

PRAYER: Thank God that you both have needs only the other can meet. Pray for the wisdom to meet those needs fairly with mutual concern for one another.

ACTION: Having devotions about sex can draw you closer or possibly start up the Crazy Cycle. Share honestly with each other about your needs on this two-way street. Talk together or possibly write each other notes about your needs as lovingly and respectfully as you can. If sex continues to be a serious issue, consider seeing a skilled Christian counselor. See appendix D (page 289) for counseling resources. (For discussion questions, see page 235 in appendix A.)

CHAPTER 21

Keep Your Eyes on the Lord, Not the Problem

2 CHRONICLES 20:12:

*O our God. . . . We are powerless before this great
multitude who are coming against us; nor do we know
what to do, but our eyes are on You.*

Today's scripture passage may suggest a familiar situation. You feel powerless before some problem ranging from serious to overwhelming. Marriage has a way of bringing us the "what do we do now?" moments, and no answers immediately come to mind. We don't know what to do with a rebellious child, a medical report revealing cancer, more debt than income, an ailing parent, job loss—the list can be endless.

But you never have to feel totally powerless. Look at the rest of the verse: "but our eyes are on You." The man who uttered these words had big problems indeed. Jehoshaphat was king of Judah at a time when several enemy nations were gathered to march on Jerusalem and obliterate every Israelite they could find.

But Jehoshaphat had already made the first right move: he had gathered the nation of Judah together to pray, and after acknowledging to the Lord that he really had no clue about what to do, he added, "but our eyes are on You."

You can read on in 2 Chronicles 20 to see how Judah was delivered from the hands of its enemies because the people knew "the battle is not yours, but God's" (v. 15 NIV). There are rich truths in this story for every Love & Respect couple. Be aware that these "what do we do now?" moments can cause friction and tension between you. Gazing at the problem with anxiety and worry can result in unloving or disrespectful behavior. In short, you can get on the Crazy Cycle just like that.

> INSIGHT: Every day our eyes are on something. Is it the Lord or the problem?

Don't let the problem get your eyes off the Lord! In chapter 11 we learned that when a Pink wife and a Blue husband come together through the Love & Respect Connection, they become "one" and take on God's royal color of Purple. This is the time to draw together as a real team, a team that wears Purple and can deal with that problem with strength and insight. Will the problem just go away? Not likely. Things don't always turn out the way we would wish. For example, reflect on James, the brother of John, in contrast to Peter. Herod imprisoned both, but God allowed Herod to behead James (Acts 12:2), whereas an angel released Peter from the prison (Acts 12:7). Keep in mind that God remains sovereign, controlling the outcome, while our job is to keep our eyes on Him.

The apostle Paul faced all kinds of problems and hopeless situations. Recalling one of his missionary journeys, Paul says, "We were crushed and overwhelmed . . . and we thought we would never live through it . . . But as a result, we stopped rely-ing on ourselves and learned to rely only on God" (2 Corinthians 1:8–9 NLT). Paul learned again and again what it was like to feel powerless, knowing he could not trust himself. He learned not only to glance at problems but also to gaze on the Lord, fixing his eyes on Jesus. At the moment, you may or may not be facing circumstances that seem to render you powerless, but every day is an opportunity to trust the Lord. As a Purple Love & Respect couple, start every day by saying, "Our eyes are on You!"

PRAYER: If you are facing no big problems, thank the Lord. If you are facing something that appears overwhelming, confess that you are powerless, that you don't know what to do, but that your eyes are on the Lord. Praise Him, knowing the battle is not yours, but His. (You may want to bring up problems you're having at work, at church, or in other outside settings that can affect you at home.)

ACTION: Step back and look at problems (or that big problem) facing you right now. How much of this is in your control? How much are you trusting God? Lots of problems are not overwhelming, but they are big enough to draw our attention away from the Lord. Also, take inventory on love and respect. Are you gazing at problems so intently that you are forgetting about unconditional love for her, unconditional respect for him? (For discussion questions, see page 236 in appendix A.)

CHAPTER 22

Our "Good" May Be Willing, but Our Flesh Can Be Weak

ROMANS 7:18:

For I have the desire to do what is good,
but I cannot carry it out (NIV).

L ike you and your spouse, Sarah and I are committed to practicing the principle of goodwill in our marriage (see chapter 3). No matter what happens, we will look for goodwill in each other. And we intend to do good toward each other every way we can, as often as we can.

But our intentions are one thing; reality is another. Intending to show goodwill does not guarantee good choices. As Sarah's husband, I know I should be a servant of Christ and do anything and everything for her with a joyful spirit and without concern for myself. When we pray together at the start of our day, I resolve to be a loving spouse, but before nightfall I can find myself coming across to Sarah in a manner that feels unloving to her.

For example, Sarah knows I hate to shop for clothes, so she tries to simplify my life by buying three new shirts, a jacket, and slacks and bringing them home. But when she asks me to take a few minutes to try them on and decide which items I like, I get irritated. After all, I am busy writing about love and respect. I do not have time for this. As I head for the bedroom to try on the clothes, I show my aggravation, and Sarah feels very unloved for only trying to be a help to me. What happened to my early-morning good intentions to be a loving man?

> INSIGHT: The human spirit is willing and the flesh is weak, but the Holy Spirit is all-powerful.

Sarah experiences the same thing. She gets up in the morning wanting to honor Christ and show me respect, but out of the blue her good intentions go astray. In my typically preoccupied state, I do not seem to be aware of how our daughter, Joy, is bearing the brunt of helping several people she knows who have made very bad choices. Stung by my denseness, Sarah succumbs to overstating her concerns in a rather disrespectful way: "Why don't you *say* something? Ask her if you can help? What if she died? How would you feel about not talking to her about this heavy burden when you had the chance?" After laying a guilt trip on me, Sarah is soon wallowing in guilt of her own because of her outburst. She has allowed her anger to belie the goodwill and respect she felt for me at the start of the day.

At times like these, both of us identify with the apostle Paul's lament in Romans 7:18: "For I have the desire to do what is good, but I cannot carry it out." We also think of Jesus' words to His disciples when they fell asleep while He prayed in the Garden of Gethsemane: "The spirit is willing, but the flesh is weak" (Matthew 26:41).

So what do Sarah and I do? Whenever we fail to show each other love or respect, we say something like this: "You know I have goodwill, don't you? Please forgive me. I blew it again." And the one on the receiving end of the apology might respond: "I forgive you. I know you have goodwill, but you certainly can be frustrating at times."

Because Sarah and I know the road to the Crazy Cycle can be paved with good intentions, we remind each other of our desire to show goodwill. Putting our goodwill on the table, so to speak, is a good motivator to walk the walk, not just talk the talk. We never use our good intentions as an excuse to make light of bad actions. We confess our sin and trust Christ to empower our good intentions and turn them into good actions—into love and respect.

PRAYER: Thank God for His clear instructions in Romans 7 about how to deal with failing to fulfill good intentions. Ask Him for the wisdom to do marriage His way, always communicating goodwill toward each other, always being willing to seek forgiveness when falling short. Don't allow pride to put you on the Crazy Cycle!

ACTION: Take time separately to list ways you see your good intentions going awry on occasion. Exchange lists and talk about how to help each other fulfill good intentions. (For discussion questions, see page 237 in appendix A.)

CHAPTER 23

EXCUSE ME, IS THAT YOUR FOOT ON MY AIR HOSE?

ECCLESIASTES 10:12:

A wise person's words win favors, but a fool's lips are self-destructive (GW).

As I talked with a very successful businessman who had been married forty-two years, he mentioned an occasion when his wife came at him verbally in a very disrespectful way. He could have fired right back, but he chose to use what he had learned from Love & Respect, so he said, "Honey, did I do something or say something that felt unloving to you? As Emerson says, maybe I stepped on your air hose. I don't want to get on the Crazy Cycle. Tell me, did I do something that was unloving?"

In this instance his wife apologized and admitted it was her fault. They avoided the Crazy Cycle when he used the little code phrase, "maybe I stepped on your air hose," to try to find out what he had done to be unloving. Of all the tools in the L&R kit, there is none more useful than the air hose.

As I say, a wife has an air hose connected to a love tank, and she needs love like she needs air to breathe. When her husband steps on her air hose, she deflates in the face of feeling unloved. On the other hand, a husband has an air hose connected to a respect tank, and he needs respect like he needs air to breathe. When his wife steps on his air hose, he deflates in the face of feeling disrespected.

Stepping on air hoses happens in the best of marriages, and we do it in different ways, the chief of which is how we use words. To paraphrase today's verse, a wise person's words of love and respect win favors, but a fool's unloving and disrespectful words are self-destructive, not benefitting that person one iota.

Ironically, it's easy to step on your spouse's air hose without really trying. A discussion turns into a slight disagreement, which escalates into a real difference of opinion (argument). Back and forth it goes, with foolish speech flying thick and fast, as one or both air hoses get trampled in the process.

> INSIGHT: The air hose is not just a gimmick; it is a powerful God-centered tool.

It need not be, but what can a couple do when they find themselves on the edge of the Crazy Cycle (perhaps just after leading a small group discussion in their home on Love & Respect)? People tell me how they use the word picture of air hoses to relieve the tension and communicate their needs to each other. In Love & Respect (page 306) I teach wives to say, "That felt unloving. Did I just come across as disrespectful?" And I teach husbands to say, "That felt disrespectful. Did I just come across as unloving?"

I hear from L&R couples who tell me they want to ask these questions, but somehow it is a bit awkward. It is much easier to say, "Excuse me, but is that your foot on my air hose?" or per-haps, "Honey, I detect I may have just stepped on your air hose. Am I right?" Once the ice is broken, it is easier to talk about who is feeling unloved or disrespected.

Some spouses don't even have to use words. One husband told me that his wife chooses to say emphatically, "You're stomp-ing on my air hose!" but he prefers to just grab his throat and act like he is choking. Either way, they each get the message and are able to exchange wise and pleasant words like, "I am sorry. I didn't mean to do that. Please forgive me."

Solomon was right! Wise words win approval, but foolish words are destructive. How odd yet encouraging that when we use this simple word picture, good things happen. As one couple told me, "We watched for the signals when either of us might be stepping on the other's air hose, and our relationship was literally revolutionized."

Among many, many more couples, may the revolution begin!

PRAYER: Thank God for simple word pictures that can help you show each other love and respect. Ask Him for the wisdom to discern when you are stepping on each other's air hose and the courage to speak up even when it may be a bit difficult.

ACTION: When your spouse deflates before your eyes, don't defend yourself by saying, "That's your problem." Remember, it's always "our problem," and try to find out how and why an air hose is getting pinched. (For discussion questions, see page 238 in appendix A.)

CHAPTER 24

IT'S HARD TO BE NEGATIVE WHILE BEING THANKFUL

1 THESSALONIANS 5:18:

*In everything give thanks; for this is God's will
for you in Christ Jesus.*

On a scale of 1 to 10 (10 being "extremely"), how thankful are you for each other? Giving thanks comes more easily when things are going well. Trouble is, life doesn't always go that well. Yet today's verse says to give thanks in *everything* (the good and the bad and even the ugly), for it is all part of God's will for you in Christ Jesus. No one has taught me more about how to live this verse than Sarah. What I so admire is that she is thankful for me and the rest of the family because she can look beyond us and thank God. One of her favorite verses is Psalm 50:23: "He who offers a sacrifice of thanksgiving honors Me." She shares the following from her journal:

I remember when our son, David, had broken his leg quite severely while playing baseball in the eighth grade. As I saw his heart breaking over the loss of his dream to play in the major leagues someday, I realized I could not fix his leg or his dream. Now my heart was breaking also. How would I get through this? Then God showed me this wasn't a crisis with my son, but a crisis of faith for me. I knew it was God's will that I give thanks in all things, but this didn't feel like something for which to be thankful. And that is when I learned about a "sacrifice of thanksgiving" in Psalm 50:23. A sacrifice is just that, a sacrifice. Since then, I have chosen to give thanks when I don't see the good.

When I came upon this verse while David was recuperating, at first it didn't sound like a natural thing to do. But then I thought of Abraham, who was asked to sacrifice his only son on the altar. That wasn't a very natural thing to do either. I realized that sometimes we have to offer a sacrifice of thanksgiving even when things are not going well.

INSIGHT: We do the will of God when we are thankful.

That was the first of many more times in my life when I would offer a sacrifice of praise and thanksgiving. It was like a pregame warm-up with many practices in between. Little did I know I was practicing for the big game yet to come—the day I would hear the words *breast cancer*. I still gave thanks during my breast cancer and double mastectomy. Each time I offered thanksgiving as a sacrifice, I knew I was honoring God. Even though my circumstances did not always change, something was happening in the heavens *and* something was happening in my soul!

Today Sarah is cancer free. A huge display of her paraphrase of 1 Thessalonians 5:18 is on our kitchen wall:

IN ALL THINGS GIVE THANKS

She continues to offer her sacrifice of thanksgiving with praise and worship, and this releases her faith and provides her with confidence in God's love and care. She knows that He is working even if she cannot see it.

She encourages anyone going through a time of suffering or confusion to offer God a sacrifice of thanksgiving. The application to marriage is clear. Sometimes we make our sacrifice of thanksgiving in the face of something that is less than perfect or maybe just plain bad, month after month, year after year, with no apparent change or improvement and certainly no miracle. Then it's easy to get negative about your spouse, your kids—even yourself! Don't fall into this trap. Keep thanking God, no matter what, because it's hard to be negative while being thankful.

Whatever cycle your marriage is in right now—Crazy, Energizing, or Rewarded*—I urge you to use Sarah's approach to your circumstances. Through it all—the good, the not so good, or maybe the 20 percent of trouble that is bound to come along—look beyond your circumstances to God. *That* is what being thankful is all about!

---

* If you are unfamiliar with the Rewarded Cycle, see appendix B, page 278.

PRAYER: Thank the Lord for all the positive, good things in your marriage (you may want to make a list). Also thank Him for all the troubling moments by offering up a sacrifice of thanksgiving in the face of challenges and bad news. Ask the Lord to make you a thankful Love & Respect couple—in every circumstance.

ACTION: During times of prayer together this week, offer a sacrifice of thanksgiving and praise. Introduce the practice of giving thanks whenever you pray, always aware that this is God's will for you in Christ Jesus. (For discussion questions, see page 240 in appendix A.)

CHAPTER 25

Don't Believe Everything
Your Spouse Says
(Especially in Anger)

PROVERBS 14:15:

*The gullible believe anything they're told; the prudent sift
and weigh every word* (MSG).

E arly in our marriage Sarah would say in a little-girl, pout-
ing manner, "You don't love me!" This usually caught me
off guard, sending me into stonewalling mode, and we
rode the Crazy Cycle. Finally I asked her, "Why do you say
that?" She replied, "Well, I didn't mean it the way you heard it."

That remark puzzled me. "You don't love me" sounded like
"You don't love me," to me. It took quite a while for me to really
grasp that what Sarah meant was, "I am feeling insecure; please
tell me you love me."

We constantly hear from couples who are learning that they
can't always take at face value remarks made in haste or in an

emotional moment. Such remarks are usually not meant literally as a condemning judgment. Often they are cries for help or understanding. To make it even more complicated, body language and tone of voice play a big part. At times the gentlest wife can sound shrill and have a look on her face full of contempt. And the most loving husband can have moments when he sounds harsh and the look on his face just seems angry.

If we were in perfect control of ourselves, we would keep our cool much better (James 1:19) and not speak foolishly or in haste (Proverbs 20:29). The best of us, however, can get frustrated and upset and blurt out things we don't mean, words we wish we could take back later.

INSIGHT: What is being said isn't always what is meant, and what is meant isn't always being said. Decode!

That is why it is wise not to necessarily believe everything your spouse says, especially when he or she is angry or frustrated. In many cases, the wife is simply asking for reassurance that her husband loves her; the husband is simply asking for a little more respect. My e-mail box is full of messages describing these scenarios.

One husband wrote to say that before hearing of Love & Respect, he and his wife would have recurring meltdowns. Feeling unloved, she would accuse him of "never" or "always" doing this or that, and he would respond by doing his best to hurt her back. What he now recognizes as the Crazy Cycle would happen again and again. Then they attended an L&R conference:

If I took one thing from your program, it was "decode, decode," always remembering that Jackie is a goodwilled woman—my partner. Now (and I admit I don't always get it), I hear her pleas for love as a desire to draw near to me, to connect. Inevitably, my loving response—either attempting to understand her or sharing something of my day—results in an extremely affirming message from her.

Bingo! He gets it!

And a wife writes to share how she decoded:

A couple of weeks ago we had a terrible fight and my husband yelled, "You don't respect me!" We kept at it, and he wound up in the basement sobbing in frustration. I finally realized he wasn't judging and condemning me. He really did need something from me that I was not giving him.

Bingo again!

These examples may sound a bit extreme, but even for more well-adjusted couples, it is easy to come across to each other in an unloving or disrespectful way. I believe today's Scripture passage is telling married people not to be gullible (as I was early in our marriage) and take everything they say to each other at face value. Prudently sift and weigh those heated or hasty words. Find out what your mate is *really* trying to say. It works for Sarah and me, and it can work for you!

PRAYER: Ask the Lord to help you decipher the real meaning behind each other's words, especially when one or both of you is upset. Ask Him, too, for guidance in softening your tone and look so you convey to each other what you both so deeply want—the reassurance of love and respect.

ACTION: Be willing to look behind statements like, "You don't love me," or "You don't respect me" (or words to that effect). Don't hear these comments as condemning accusations but as invitations to encourage and reassure. As a mature person, say, "Honey, I really do love you. Forgive me for not showing it as I should," or "Please believe I am not trying to be disrespectful. Please forgive me for sounding like it." (For discussion questions, see page 241 in appendix A.)

CHAPTER 26

FORGIVENESS, PART I: LOVE & RESPECT TAKES TWO GOOD FORGIVERS

COLOSSIANS 3:13:

Make allowances for each other's faults and forgive anyone who offends you. Remember, the Lord forgave you, so you must forgive others (NLT).

R uth Graham, whose marriage to Billy lasted over sixty happy, God-glorifying years, was often heard to say, "A good marriage is made of two good forgivers." Her comment, while true for every marriage, applies especially to a Love & Respect couple, because forgiveness is the ultimate strategy for halting the Crazy Cycle or, better yet, for preventing it from getting started. A paraphrase of today's verse says it all: forgive each other as Christ forgave you.

We know we should forgive, but between the knowing and the doing there can be a big gap. And when you are sitting on the unforgiving side of that gap, you can pay a price. Jesus warned

His followers of how big that price can be when He taught, "If you refuse to forgive others, your Father will not forgive your sins" (Matthew 6:15 NLT).

Was Jesus saying that unforgiveness could cost you your salvation? No, but it can disrupt your fellowship and favor with the Lord. God does not damn us for unforgiveness, but He does enact discipline. Sarah and I learned this early in our marriage, when a typical morning scene would find us in an angry spat,

INSIGHT: To not forgive is to shoot yourself in the foot and put extra gas in the Crazy Cycle.

neither one willing to forgive or ask forgiveness. Still smoldering, I would leave for my office at the church to work on my sermon for the coming Sunday. But when I sat down to pray and read the Scriptures, the heavens would not open. God seemed to have something on His mind. I heard no audible voice, but He spoke quite clearly nonetheless: *If you do not forgive Sarah and seek her forgiveness, I cannot allow My Spirit to touch your spirit. Things will not be right until you call her and reconcile.*

More often than not, I would reach for the phone to make that call and it would ring first. It would be Sarah, wanting to reconcile because she had been getting exactly the same message from the Lord!

Our spats were usually small stuff—two young married people butting heads over very little. Our conflicts were nothing compared to what some couples go through due to adultery, abuse, or desertion. But whether the matter is major or minor, the path to forgiveness is to realize that the issue that prompts your need to forgive isn't primarily about your relationship to your spouse; it's about your relationship to God. Suppose Sarah is 100 percent guilty in wronging me. Her guilt cannot justify my unforgiving heart. I can remain unforgiving of Sarah as long as I wish. While I lick my wounds, I can argue with God and explain my "right" to be unforgiving. But God's spiritual law stands firm: if I don't forgive, I remain in a place where God's forgiveness will not go because sin blocks our fellowship.

Do you remember the scene where Peter comes to Jesus, wanting to know how many times he must forgive? He gives an estimate that he hopes will impress Jesus: seven times. That was twice what the law required, but Jesus simply replies, "Not seven times, but seventy-seven times" (Matthew 18:22 NIV). His hyperbole makes the message clear to every couple—*forgive indefinitely.*

Granted, right about here you may be asking, okay, Emerson, to be right with God, does forgiving mean just letting the same hurtful, unloving, or disrespectful stuff go by over and over without ever talking about it?

No, not at all, but that's part II of our study of forgiveness (see chapter 27). For now, focus on the fact that your Love & Respect marriage does take two good forgivers. You make allowance for each other's faults as you forgive as many times as it takes. And you both forgive for one simple but profound reason: *because you know Christ has forgiven you!*

PRAYER: Thank God for forgiving you through the sacrifice of His son. Ask Him for the wisdom and courage to forgive each other seventy times or as many times as it takes. (Also consider bringing up people whom you need to forgive at work, at church, or in other situations, because these issues could be affecting how you treat your spouse or children.)

ACTION: Practice "quick forgiveness" this week no matter what the offense. Don't let "little things" fester. Pick up that phone and make that call. (For discussion questions, see page 242 in appendix A.)

CHAPTER 27

FORGIVENESS, PART II: GOT FORGIVENESS? LET JESUS BE YOUR MODEL

1 PETER 2:21:

*Christ suffered for you. He is your example,
and you must follow in His steps (NLT).*

In chapter 26 we looked at some basics on forgiveness: we must forgive or our fellowship with the Lord will be broken, and we must continue to forgive, over and over again—marriage takes two good forgivers. But there is more to it than that. A question I hear continually is, exactly *how* do I forgive when the hurts go deep, when I am still smarting from no love or no respect?

The apostle Peter gives us a good place to start in today's key verse. Make Jesus your example and follow in His steps (1 Peter 2:21). We get the same idea from the writer of Hebrews, who tells us to put aside what can trip us up and run the race marked out for us, by fixing our eyes on Jesus, who endured the cross for us (see Hebrews 12:1–2).

If anyone was hurt deeply, it was Jesus. I see Him doing two things to forgive, and they are things we can do, too, as we follow in His steps:

1. Sympathize with your spouse (try to understand what is causing the hurtful behavior).
2. Relinquish the offense to God (let it go; don't let resentment fester in your soul).

Sympathizing with your spouse may not be the first thing on your mind if you are the one who has been offended, but consider how Jesus responded to horrible mistreatment with patient forgiveness as He prayed from the cross: "Father, forgive them, for they do not know what they are doing" (Luke 23:34 NIV). Jesus forgave the Jewish mob and the Roman soldiers by looking beyond their heinous crime to see the ignorance, mindless fear, and blind hatred that was driving them.

Although the slights and offenses suffered in marriage are trifling by comparison, you can follow Jesus' example in principle when your spouse offends you deliberately or unknowingly in any number of mundane ways that seem to be part of marriage. How? By trying to understand what might be causing the impatience, rudeness, or lack of consideration. Perhaps bad habits learned while growing up have surfaced; maybe the cause is stress from work or from dealing with the kids' problems, or maybe it is fear of what one of you might think or say. The list can go on and on.

But trying to identify the problem is only a start. You can't stop there. You need to talk about what has been happening. Express your hurt, but do it civilly and tactfully. Perhaps you simply need to let someone know your air hose is getting seriously pinched (review chapter 23). Or it could be time to speak a difficult truth with love and respect (review chapter 15). In all such conversations you know you can follow the example of Jesus because you are married to a person who has basic goodwill and does not intend to hurt you (see chapters 3 and 22).

As you sort out your feelings together, remember that you cannot expect success if you come to the "negotiating table" begrudgingly. To get somewhere there must be a forgiving spirit present—obviously in the one who feels wronged, but also in the one who has done the offending and may be feeling defensive or have reasons to feel offended also. Truth be told, you both may have some forgiving to do before it is over.

And do not neglect to relinquish the offense. Give your pain and frustration to God. Refuse to hang on to remnants of an unforgiving spirit. Yes, I know the hurt may still linger, but trust God to help you let it all go. When Jesus suffered, He "kept entrusting Himself to Him who judges righteously" (1 Peter 2:23), and you can do the same in the midst of lesser difficulties.

> **INSIGHT:** To get offended is easy, but to forgive is within your power, as you walk in His steps.

When you sympathize with your spouse, you will tend to speak with understanding and compassion instead of anger and judgment. As you entrust your "wounds" to the Lord, you will lower your expectations for total healing from your spouse, and that will create a calmness and wisdom in your approach. Will you kiss and make up? Perhaps, but most important, Jesus has been your example. You have followed in His steps!

PRAYER: Thank the Lord Jesus for His example of how to forgive. Ask Him for the wisdom and grace to try to understand, and then let it go.

ACTION: Forgiving truly hurtful offenses is a delicate area. If you have issues of this kind, come together and talk about how to confront the situation (not just each other). You may want to review chapter 16, "Feelings Aren't Facts—Always Sort It Out," as well as the chapters previously mentioned. If one spouse feels very hurt, the other must reach out to understand. Talk together with God, asking for His help while addressing the hurt. (For discussion questions, see page 243 in appendix A.)

CHAPTER 28

No Matter How You Feel, Trust Scripture More Than Your Feelings

1 CORINTHIANS 13:11:

*When we were children, we thought and reasoned as children do.
But when we grew up, we quit our childish ways* (CEV).

A ny husband and wife will agree that marriage is a cru-
cible of emotions and feelings, some ecstatic, some good,
some bad or indifferent. But a marriage cannot survive
on feelings alone. Feelings are supposed to be tempered by ratio-
nal thinking, by common sense, and, yes, in a Christian marriage,
by asking, what does the Bible say?

Billy Graham, arguably the best-known and most effective
evangelist of all time, was famous for saying, "The Bible says . . ."
It was his trademark as he preached to over two billion people
during his career, and it was his credo at home with Ruth, his
wife and soul mate of almost sixty-four years. Billy and Ruth

had what many called a model marriage, filled with his love for her and her respect for him and the ministry to which God had called him. She was his number-one adviser and critic, as well as his companion and confidant, lover and friend. She spent many days and hours alone parenting their five children and running their home while Billy was on a crusade. He freely admitted that without her unconditional support he could not have done what God called him to do.

I have no doubt that Billy and Ruth Graham had such a strong marriage because God's Word came first, ahead of their own feelings. They went against the popular tide that says feelings rule and emotions justify actions. During more than thirty-five years of marriage counseling, I have listened to many husbands and wives who balk at the idea of not giving their feelings full reign, Bible or no Bible. For example: "But Emerson, my feelings are *real!* Are you telling me to deny my feelings, like anger at my spouse? You and Sarah get angry at each other, don't you?"

INSIGHT: Feelings can be wrong. What the Bible says is always right.

To this I reply, "True enough. Our feelings are always real to us, but that doesn't always make them right in God's eyes." Whatever the emotion, Scripture must override our sinful sentiments.

Some very real feelings can be very wrong. I used to throw temper tantrums on the floor. Those feelings were real, but I eventually stopped (I think it was my second year in seminary). I got perspective. I realized that what upset me wasn't as bad as I thought or imagined. Paul put it perfectly in today's passage: "When we were children, we thought and reasoned as children do. But when we grew up, we quit our childish ways" (1 Corinthians 13:11; see also 1 Corinthians 14:20).

Paul also teaches believers to "become mature," to "grow up" and become like the One they profess to follow (Ephesians 4:13–15 NCV). This is at the very heart of Love & Respect. Ever since Sarah and I started this ministry, we have sought to help married couples (including ourselves) become more mature in Christ and to grow up to be the people He wants us all to be. We have received literally hundreds of letters over the years from husbands and wives who testify to how Love & Respect—through the books or through a conference—has brought the power of God's Word into their lives.

One man, married over thirty years, read *Love & Respect* and *The Language of Love & Respect*, and besides the Scripture, for him the best parts were the letters and testimonials, plus the experiences Sarah and I share of our own struggles and steps of faith. As he read, he was able to see real people experiencing the power and truth of God's Word. He writes: "It was like reading about modern-day heroes of the faith who trust God no matter what, believe that He is who He says He is, and believe His promises. That is so motivating and encouraging! Real people, with the real grace of God poured into their lives and as they first believe Christ, follow Him in complete obedience, no matter what is being communicated, the emotions they experience, or the circumstances they're in."

This man gets it. His words about obeying Christ "no matter what" say it all. Feelings are real, yes, but in a Love & Respect marriage, God's Word trumps feelings every time.

THE LOVE AND RESPECT DEVOTIONAL

PRAYER: Ask the Lord for wisdom in dealing with feelings, no matter how right or real they may seem. Thank Him for any progress you have made in growing up into Christ as you practice love and respect.

ACTION: Whatever comes up this week, ask: I know how I feel, but what does Scripture say? (For discussion questions, see page 244 in appendix A.)

CHAPTER 29

REMEMBER, GOD DESIGNED YOUR SPOUSE—BE PATIENT!

EPHESIANS 4:1–2:

Walk in a manner worthy of the calling with which you have been called, with all humility and gentleness, with patience, showing tolerance for one another in love.

How do you feel about how God designed your spouse? We know we are as different as Pink and Blue (see chapter 2), but there is a lot more to it than that. Whether Pink or Blue, your spouse is a unique design of gifts, temperament, and passions. You fell in love with that design, but perhaps you have discovered it is not perfect after all. For some reason, there are times when you can get annoyed, irritated, or even angry when your spouse is simply being the person God made in the first place. At moments like these, we all need patience, a quality we all agree is important. We often say we are praying for patience while we secretly wish God would hurry up and send a big dose fast!

In Ephesians 4:1-2 the apostle Paul urges Christ followers to combine humility and gentleness with patience, which will lead to showing tolerance and acceptance of each other's differences. It is this kind of patience that empowers Pink and Blue to appreciate how God designed each of them—especially during those moments when they might provoke and annoy one another.

I never cease to marvel at how God has designed Sarah and me so differently. Years ago our temperaments and individual gifts caused some needless friction because we were intolerant of our different approaches to a situation. For example, Sarah is empathic, focusing on the person with the problem, and I am analytical, focusing on the problem the person has. She wonders why I seem so uncaring at times, and I wonder why she gets so emotional. But as we have become a real team, we have learned to be accepting and appreciative of our individual and unique designs. Patience with each other has descended on our marriage—most of the time!

INSIGHT: God designed your spouse just for you. Be patient.

Like any other couple, we must still work at being gentle and accepting and be aware of what happens when impatience rears its intolerant head. And, not surprisingly, we have learned that when one of us has a need, it can irritate the other. Sarah may be crying out for love when she speaks hastily with intense feeling, but she does not mean to be disrespectful. When I raise my voice to authoritatively make my point, I am feeling in need of a little more respect, but I do not mean to be unloving. And so it goes. Opportunities to be patient with each other abound each day.

I like this wife's words: "I am leaning on God for a lot of

patience. I pray that Jon and I will be able to figure out how we can feel loved and respected in our relationship."

To feel loved or respected—that is always the goal that seems to need a little more work each day. May I offer you a challenge? Recognize your different gifts, how each of you—Pink and Blue—functions according to God's perfect design. His Spirit will bear the fruit of patience as you humbly and gently show each other tolerance with love and respect. Stay with it, and remember: it takes a lot of patience to learn patience!

PRAYER: Thank the Lord for your individual gifts and temperaments, and ask forgiveness for your impatience. Ask for the wisdom to appreciate each other with love and respect. Also ask God for help with situations at work, at church, or in other outside settings that may try your patience and affect your interactions at home.

ACTION: This week, make a special effort to see each other from the vantage point of God's design. Realize He did not create your spouse's gifts, temperament, gender, and passions to frustrate and annoy you. Talk together about what it means to be patient with each other in different situations. (For discussion questions, see page 245 in appendix A.)

CHAPTER 30

Impact Others with Love & Respect

1 CORINTHIANS 12:6:

*God works in different ways, but it is the same God
who does the work in all of us* (NLT).

Having come this far with these devotionals, perhaps it is time to take stock of how Love & Respect is impacting your marriage. Which of the following describes you right now?

- We struggle with the Crazy Cycle, but we are hanging in there.
- We are making progress, but we have a way to go.
- We don't have it all wired yet, but we are enthused. This stuff works!
- Comments: _____

No matter how you rate your marriage at the moment, I want to challenge you to think about sharing what has impacted you so far. I know of many couples who might be struggling with building a biblical marriage, but they have still opened their homes and have profited from sharing this message with others who struggle too.

If this teaching has affected your marriage to any degree at all, it could be time to start spreading the L&R word. How? Perhaps you could get a set of the DVDs of the conference (www .loveandrespect.com), and invite several couples over to watch the first session. What often happens is that some of those you invite will want to keep going and watch the whole series. You don't have to be Love & Respect experts to facilitate a small group—just be open and enthusiastic. Look at it as a win-win. No matter where you are in your own marriage—struggling or making real progress—going over these principles with other couples will be a huge benefit. People will respond and wonderful things can happen, as this letter describes:

> Because of our tremendous differences, our pastor asked us to facilitate your video series. God must have spoken to him because we were the least qualified to do this. In fact, I wouldn't have listened to me! But the change in us was so amazing that 80 percent of our church came. Three of these couples were headed toward litigation . . . people are feeling loved for the first time in their lives!

We get letter after letter like this. Here's what one husband reported after hosting a group in his home:

> Well, it went over so well that our pastor got a copy of *Love & Respect* and did a sermon on it. He asked if my wife and I would be willing to be interviewed before the whole church in

support of this program. We agreed and even had fun with it. Here's what has come out of it: we are being asked to facilitate this seminar on DVD for other small groups. We also are doing private showings for two couples whose marriages are in very bad shape, and other churches are asking us to host a DVD seminar for them.

Do stories like these excite you, intimidate you, or maybe a little bit of both? One way to explain today's key verse is that there are different kinds of gifts and abilities that can become different kinds of ministries that will have different results (see 1 Corinthians 12:4–6). Is God asking you to open your home to other couples or even present this material in a Sunday school class? Or here's a thought: What about organizing a Love & Respect video conference for your entire church and other churches in your community?

INSIGHT: If we are profiting from Love & Respect, perhaps it is time to share the wealth.

What do you need to do? Just step out in faith. What effect will you have? As the apostle Paul puts it, God works in different ways in our lives. I don't know what impact you will have, but as you step out, just trust God to work through you for His glory. Ready. Set. Go, God!

PRAYER: Thank God for touching you with His message of love and respect. Ask Him to guide you in considering what you might do to share this message with others. If you are already doing something with a group of some kind, ask Him to work His miracles in your midst.

ACTION: This week, investigate the resources available at www .loveandrespect.com/store. As God leads, think about a setting in which you could use these resources, and invite others to join you. (For discussion questions, see page 246 in appendix A.)

CHAPTER 31

MUTUAL SUBMISSION, SEX, AND TUESDAY NIGHT

EPHESIANS 5:21:

Submit to one another out of reverence for Christ (NIV).

I t is Tuesday night (although it could be any night of the week). John has been under a lot of stress at work and feels the need for the kind of release only Mary can provide. After dinner John broaches the subject but gets a rather unenthusiastic look from Mary, who has been up to her hips in baby alligators all day. At this point the scenario can play out in different ways: (1) John feels rebuffed and stonewalls Mary the rest of the evening. (2) Mary gives in but feels used and not at all fulfilled as John satisfies his urge. (3) They work it out, using the principles of mutual submission in Ephesians 5:21.

Mutual submission? I can remember earlier in our marriage praying, *Lord, how do Sarah and I mutually submit to each other when I am called to be the head?* God's inaudible voice spoke to my heart: *Mutual submission is less about specific decisions and more about attitude.*

You submit to Sarah's need for love out of reverence for Me, and she submits to your need for respect out of reverence for Me. No matter the disagreement, you can both display love and respect and thereby meet the other's deepest need. This is mutual submission out of reverence for Me. I realized that by practicing love and respect, mutual submission is possible.

> **INSIGHT:** Mutual submission is the only way to live fairly together with mutual authority.

Sounds like a good theory, but can it work on Tuesday night? John wants sex; Mary is exhausted and not in the mood. Mutual submission seems impossible—or is it? In chapter 20 we looked at sex and affection as a two-way street. Typically a husband's primary need is sex, and a wife's primary need is affection and emotional connection. Note that I said "typically." I get numerous e-mails from *wives* who want more sexual intimacy; their husbands are depriving *them!* But the principle Paul lays down in 1 Corinthians 7:3 stands: *both spouses should seek to be fair, giving each other what is due.*

And in 1 Corinthians 7:4, Paul spells out the connection between sex, affection, and mutual submission: "The wife does not have authority over her own body, but the husband does; and likewise also the husband does not have authority over his own body, but the wife does." Mutual authority leads to mutual submission.

How? Well, John can respond to Mary's no on Tuesday with understanding (if not disappointment), and she can suggest waiting until Wednesday, when she will be leaving the kids with Grandma for the evening. The key is communicating, working it out. I liken it to riding a teeter-totter. Though the teeter-totter experience feels unfair to someone on any given night, over time

John and Mary can experience a sense of balance. As they walk the two-way street—sex for him, affection for her—they create equilibrium through mutual submission.

The goodwilled couple (see chapters 3 and 22) can work this sex and affection issue out, keeping some basic thoughts in mind:

- Always remember that Pink and Blue have different wiring, different preferences. Assume your spouse has goodwill toward you no matter what. Both of you can be right, while being different.
- As you seek to mutually submit, avoid like the plague trying to punish each other as a means of "motivation." Christ followers instinctively know that this destroys any opportunity to act out of reverence for Christ. In all marital issues, love and reverence for Christ must be our primary motivation.

Take the risk and admit your vulnerabilities to each other. If sex or affection is missing in a marriage, somebody is depriving somebody else. Paul knew the dangers in this and advised the Corinthians to stop depriving each other, except by mutual agreement, but to come back together "so that Satan will not tempt you because of your lack of self-control" (1 Corinthians 7:5 NIV). However, when expressing your own need and vulnerability, be sure to express your desire to understand and meet your spouse's need. And remember, *you are friends*, and friends always seek to mutually understand each other.

The Lord is Master in the master bedroom. He has given husband and wife mutual authority, and by implication He calls for mutual submission. Work it out together wisely, with love and respect.

PRAYER: Thank the Lord that He has given the two of you equal say in matters like sex and affection. Thank Him, too, that you have goodwill toward each other, even though you may have different needs and preferences. Ask Him for wisdom in finding the right balance through mutual submission.

ACTION: When tension arises over desires for sex and affection, refuse to judge each other as wrong. Talk it out *as friends*, seeking to understand each other's needs. If sex continues to be a serious issue, consider seeing a skilled Christian counselor. See appendix D (page 289) for counseling resources. (For discussion questions, see page 247 in appendix A.)

CHAPTER 32

ANGER CAN BE DANGEROUS . . . HANDLE WITH CARE

EPHESIANS 4:26–27:

"In your anger do not sin": Do not let the sun go down while you are still angry, and do not give the devil a foothold (NIV).

I n chapter 28 we looked at always subjecting our emotions and "real" feelings to the rule of Scripture. Instead of growling at each other ("Let me tell *you* a thing or three!"), we seek to be loving, respectful, and certainly mature adults who try to do what the Bible says.

Christian maturity involves a lot of things, but surely it includes knowing how to process your anger. In fact, I believe there is no more dangerous emotion for a married couple to deal with than anger. The apostle Paul did not teach that all anger is wrong, but that it's what you do with your anger that counts. "'In your anger,'" writes Paul, "'do not sin': Do not let the sun go down while you are still angry" (Ephesians 4:26). You have probably heard these familiar words in more than one sermon. The question is, how can you use Paul's instructions as you practice Love & Respect? Paul knew that to have real feelings is very human, but to let real feelings turn into hard feelings that rage on is childish and dangerous. When anger takes control, the Devil is ready to move in and put you on the Crazy Cycle. Satan loves the Crazy Cycle; it is his favorite mode of transportation and he wants to ride it with you!

The Devil is always scheming, and one of his favorite targets is your marriage. But there are ways to be awake and ready for Satan's schemes (Ephesians 6:11–18). For example, have you ever realized after an angry exchange, *That wasn't me. What came over me?* What came over you was the Devil. He did not possess you, but your anger gave him the opportunity to take advantage of you (2 Corinthians 2:11).

> INSIGHT: When anger is in control, sin and the Devil can have a field day.

Try to remember that during marital tension, you can easily slip into what I call "default mode," behaving in a way that reflects the human tendency to react more readily in a sinful way than a holy way. If not careful, you will follow your subjective and sinful feelings and justify these feelings because they are "so real." If you feel frustrated, you can default into sinful anger. If you feel hurt, you can default into retaliation. If you wish to "make a firm point," you can default into making a cutting remark. Justifying such feelings by calling them "righteous indignation" does not impress the Lord. What does the Bible say? "Your anger can never make things right in God's sight" (James 1:20 NLT).

Bottom line: when you default into "just being human" and feed your carnal nature, you give the Devil a foothold he wouldn't have had if you had controlled your anger. But you don't have to default; you can defeat the Devil's schemes by calling on God for help. Yes, you may have real feelings of frustration toward your mate, but you know that doesn't justify losing it emotionally or saying nasty things. Yes, you may be angry, but you choose not to sin. You have real feelings of hurt from the misunderstanding, but you know it is an honest misunderstanding, and you decide to pull back, count to ten, and give yourself time to cool off. One approach you might want to try is reading Proverbs 14:29 out loud three times (or ten, if necessary): "People with understanding control their anger; a hot temper shows great foolishness" (NLT).

Anger might be the quickest way to get on the Crazy Cycle. But as Sarah says, "We don't have to stay there." We don't deny our anger, nor do we impulsively fire away at each other. We try to find a middle ground by pulling back to defuse the anger and then moving toward each other to discuss our feelings. That way we get off the Crazy Cycle and enjoy the sunset together!

PRAYER: Ask the Lord for the wisdom to defeat Satan, the schemer who intends to gain a foothold in your marriage through sinful anger. Thank Him for any progress you have made in controlling anger and not letting real feelings turn into hard feelings.

ACTION: When I realize I'm getting angry, I will tell myself, *I will not let the sun go down on my anger.* Before I put my head on the pillow, my anger will be gone. (For discussion questions, see page 248 in appendix A.)

CHAPTER 33

All Things Do Work Together for Good . . . Sooner or Later

ROMANS 8:28:

And we know that in all things God works for the good of those who love him, who have been called according to his purpose (NIV).

W hen one of you makes a mistake, control any anger you may feel and trust God completely no matter what happens."

These words were a bit of advice I offered to my son, Jonathan, and his bride, Sarah, in a special letter I wrote to them, eighteen months after I officiated at their wedding in a storybook setting on Mackinac Island in Michigan. One of the stories I put in the letter follows. It's a story that may be hard to believe, but it is true.

Married less than a year, Sarah and I arrived at my parents' home for a weekend visit. While preparing for bed, I noticed I had forgotten my contact lens case, so I improvised (a fatal mistake). For overnight storage of my contacts, I put water in two juice glasses, dropped a contact in each, and put them on the top of the toilet tank, in a nice, "safe" place. Next morning, I found one of the glasses empty and my contact gone!

"Sarah!" I yelled. "Did you do anything with my contacts in the two juice glasses on the back of the toilet?"

When I heard "Oh, no!," I knew we had a problem. "I got up in the night and used one of those glasses to take a pill."

Mad as a hornet, I bellowed, "You did *what*?! How could you?! For heaven's sake, you DRANK my contact?!"

As Sarah joined me in the bathroom, she left the door open. Young and very much in love, we were not too skilled in handling anger. Stung by my heated words, which my parents could hear, Sarah retorted, "Why would anyone in his right mind not put a sign up saying, 'Do not use'?"

I retorted by questioning Sarah's sanity as well, wondering why anyone would drink out of a glass sitting on the back of a toilet. She wondered why anyone would leave a glass of water there if he didn't want it used. Round and round we went, making no sense. Knowing we had no money to replace the contact—an expensive item at that time—only fueled our frustration and anger.

INSIGHT: Love your Lord, then trust Him. He is working it out.

Eventually we calmed down. I felt foolish for going off on Sarah and in front of my parents to boot. Within the hour Sarah and I prayed together and we invited my parents to join us. As we both asked forgiveness for our anger, we claimed the promise in Romans 8:28—that God would cause everything to work together for good for those who love Him. My prayer was short: "Lord, You know about the contact. Your will and good work be done. Thank You."

Because we could ill afford any extra expense, I went to the optometrist fearing the worst. To keep this story short, I got the best. My eyes had always needed contacts of different strengths. The doctor's tests showed that I needed stronger contacts on both eyes, but the contact I had left was the exact strength needed for one of my eyes, so I only had to get one new contact. Sarah had swallowed the contact that needed replacing!

Sarah and I rejoiced at the good news, seeing it as a sign that God does indeed make all things work together for good for those who love Him, even the mundane stuff. But suppose I had needed two new contacts? Would God have failed to hold up His end of the "bargain" in Romans 8:28? Of course not. God does not always send happy endings that fit our perspective, but He does work out things for the good of those who love Him (and sometimes He allows contacts to be swallowed so we can truly see).

God had worked good in our lives as we learned that a good marriage is not about being perfect communicators who never lose their cool, but when we do, it's about talking to Him and listening for His answers. It's not about staying angry at each other for days over a mistake; it's about swallowing our pride, stopping to pray, and seeking God's guidance. Over the years we have learned that we stay on the right path when *we trust God completely, no matter what happens.* We urge you to do the same, knowing He does work out things for good . . . sooner or later.

PRAYER: Thank the Lord that when frustrating or bad things happen, somehow, at sometime, He works things together for good. Ask for the wisdom and faith to believe His promise in Romans 8:28.

ACTION: When bad things happen, call time out, settle down, then go to God in prayer, trusting Him to work things out for good according to His perfect timing. (For discussion questions, see page 249 in appendix A.)

CHAPTER 34

Do You Seek to Understand or Only Want to Be Understood?

Be quick to listen, slow to speak, and slow to become angry (NIV).

What, in your opinion, is the biggest problem facing most marriages today? Lack of communication or lack of mutual understanding?

A lot of people tell me their biggest problem is lack of communication. Others wonder if they can ever understand each other; some think it is impossible. As one husband said to his wife, "Well, I am Blue, and you are Pink, so get over it. I am not supposed to understand you."

Obviously he hadn't "gotten it," but fortunately his wife had, and although she was hurt by his ultra-Blue comment, she replied, "Well, honey, what I got out of Emerson's teaching was that, yes, you are Blue and I am Pink, but that means that I need to work real hard to think outside my Pink box and try to understand Blue, not that I should just discount you because you are Blue."

This wife had a handle on what I think is the bigger challenge in marriage—gaining mutual understanding. Communication is certainly an issue, and we spend a lot of time teaching about it. But as I say in *The Language of Love & Respect*, until Sarah and I understood that as a Pink she "speaks love" and as a Blue I "speak respect," we kept riding the Crazy Cycle. However, when I learned to speak Sarah's "mother tongue" of love and she learned to speak my "mother tongue" of respect, we were on our way to mutual understanding, which of course leads to better communication.

Note that I say "we were on our way." We are still not completely there, but we are making excellent progress. As we try to understand where the other is coming from by tuning our Pink and Blue hearing aids to the other's frequency, the tension evaporates. The Crazy Cycle slinks back into its cage, and we are good to go.

> INSIGHT: Be quick to listen and understand and you have a much better chance of being understood.

Another way to put it is that we have learned that it is more important to understand than be understood. Many couples remain on the Crazy Cycle to one degree or another because they keep insisting, "If you would only *understand me!*" As James 1:19, today's key verse, puts it, "Be quick to listen, slow to speak." As one spouse listens and makes the other feel understood, he or she is in a much better place to say, "I think I understand your side. Would it be okay if I explained how I see it?"

Remember, no matter what the issue under discussion is, the real issue often is love and respect. Actually, the old proverb

"You scratch my back, and I'll scratch yours" comes into play. What wife will refuse to try to understand her husband's need for respect if he first seeks to understand her need for love? And what husband will refuse to understand his wife's need for love after she seeks to understand his need for respect?

For example, a wife wrote to tell me of how her husband had made one of those Blue remarks that left her thinking, *I can't believe he said that!* Instead of getting offended, she calmly asked him what he was thinking when he said it: "I let him know that I wanted to understand what I thought I had heard him say. He clarified, and sure enough, I had heard his Blue thoughts through my Pink hearing aids. I was thrilled to see how this opened communication between us. It deepened my belief that I can talk about my feelings and get clarification without being afraid of his response."

Bingo! Instead of firing back to make sure her hurt feelings were understood, she calmly tried to understand. With one simple, calm question, this wife kept them off the Crazy Cycle and got the Energizing Cycle fired up. To paraphrase James's age-old advice, be quick to listen and understand instead of speaking your piece without getting your spouse's side of the story. Remember this little riddle: Why did God give me two ears and one mouth? He wants me to listen more than I talk!

PRAYER: Thank the Lord for two ears and one mouth. Ask Him for the wisdom to know how and when to use both. Ask for help in learning to understand first and be understood afterward.

ACTION: During conversations this week practice trying to understand first, then being understood. A good lead-in line for wanting to understand is, "What I hear you saying is . . . Am I correct?" (For discussion questions, see page 250 in appendix A.)

IT *IS* ALL ABOUT ME, AFTER ALL

ROMANS 14:12:

Yes, each of us will give a personal account to God (NLT).

L et us face it. Living up to the wedding vows you both took is not easy in this postmodern culture. The term *postmodern* involves a lot of things, but essentially it means there is no final source of absolute truth, and if there is a "creator," he is not a personal God to whom we are accountable.[1] In this kind of climate the idea of staying married as long as you both shall live has been twisted by a lot of people who cross their fingers at the wedding ceremony and think, *well, maybe as long as we both shall love.* After all, if there is no source of absolute truth to whom we must give account, who is to say how long we need to stay married, especially if love has "faded"?

Of course, Christians don't think like this, especially Love & Respect couples, so there is no problem, right? I wish it were so, but the epidemic that motivated me to start Love and

Respect Ministries in 1999 is still raging in far too many marriages. Divorce rates, in the church and out, keep going through the roof for any number of reasons, but often because "we just aren't happy together." A 2010 report in the *New York Times* on research findings regarding happy marriages highlighted the following two questions that are supposed to help you assess how happy you are.[2]

How much does your partner provide a source of exciting experiences?

How much has knowing your partner made you a better person?

Innocent enough questions? Hardly. They are perfect examples of postmodern thinking, which does not have to give an account to any kind of higher power or ultimate truth. The viewpoint behind questions like these does not ask, what's in this marriage for my spouse? Instead, the question being asked today is, what's in this marriage for *me*? Does my partner improve my life in every way by providing great conversation, wonderful companionship at Club Med, and, of course, exciting romance and sexual intimacy? Obviously, if any of these elements are average or less than average, then that must mean bits and maybe chunks of happiness are missing.

> **INSIGHT:** My marriage *is* all about me—and Jesus.

We like to think L&R couples are practically immune to this worldly "what's in this for me?" syndrome, but we all know better. We have been on the Crazy Cycle and know how easy it is to get on again. There has to be a different motivation for Christ followers, and it begins by getting the question totally straight: *What's in my marriage for Jesus?* Yes, I should want to put my spouse ahead of myself, but doing that is really a by-product of my first responsibility—to please my Lord and Savior.

As she wraps up the session she teaches at our conference, Sarah throws the crowd a bit of a curve by saying, "It's all about me . . ." And then she goes right on to explain: "It's all about me doing what God is asking me to do in relationship to my spouse." Sarah is helping everyone in the room think ahead to that day when, "Yes, each of us will give a personal account to God" (Romans 14:12). Each of us will "appear before the judgment seat of Christ" to receive what is due us (2 Corinthians 5:10 NIV).

Think of it this way. What will Jesus ask us as we stand before Him on that final day to give Him our "personal account"? He will not be asking, "What did your spouse do to make things more exciting for you?" He will be asking, "What was in your marriage for Me? Did you try to glorify Me as you did your best to unconditionally love or respect your spouse?"

The point is clear: marriage *is* all about you—it's not about trying to get your spouse to please you, but about seeking to please your Savior and Lord. And as you please Him through His grace, you will be pleased, forever and ever!

PRAYER: Thank the Lord for His grace, which not only gives salvation, but also the strength to do good works, especially in marriage. Ask Him for the wisdom to understand fully what it means to say, "My marriage *is* all about me and how I can glorify my Lord."

ACTION: For the next week or longer, put little notes up—on the mirror, cupboard door, or wherever you will see them often—saying, "It *is* all about me." Talk together about the effect this reminder has on how you treat one another. (For discussion questions, see page 251 in appendix A.)

CHAPTER 36

WHO MAKES THE FIRST MOVE IN YOUR MARRIAGE?

HEBREWS 5:14:

Solid food is for those who are mature, who through training have the skill to recognize the difference between right and wrong (NLT).

P eople always ask, "Who moves first to get off the Crazy Cycle and onto the Energizing Cycle?" I always reply, "I prayed about the answer, and I heard the Lord's inaudible voice: *the one who sees himself or herself as the most mature moves first.*"

Early on, when I shared that answer, I wondered if people would resist the idea because it suggests somebody always has to make the first move, and this doesn't sound "fair." Most of us want the other person to move first at least half the time. After many years, however, I have the confidence to say that this comment positively motivates most people. Why? Because most spouses see themselves as mature and able "to recognize the difference between right and wrong" (Hebrews 5:14).

A husband writes: "Who moves first? If it is the one who

is the most mature (and I believe that I am mature), I have no excuse. It doesn't matter who hurt first. I've shared that insight with a lot of people because of the difference it made in my conduct."

Another man says: "We have two young daughters, aged four and seven. I want to be the mature one who breaks the cycle and turns things around. I know that this is what God wills and

> INSIGHT: The mature one in the marriage seldom moves second.

what is best for my family. It is difficult and I am not perfect, but I am working to show my wife unconditional love."

A wife e-mails: "I made a decision at that moment that my life was going to count for something for the kingdom. To me, that meant learning my Bible and obeying God in my marriage and every part of my life. I am the mature one and I needed to go first. That always made me mad before, and now I am accepting that God requires it of me. God got hold of my heart that day in a way as never before."

As these letters attest, mature moves by goodwilled spouses positively influence the marriage in God's direction. But what does moving first look like? Maturity manifests itself in multiple ways. Some examples:

- During a moment of "heated fellowship," Steven softens his raised voice in response to Tanya's even louder voice. She clearly hears his olive branch.
- After Susan spouts off disrespectful words on the heels of Richard's unloving comments, she apologizes first, saying, "I am sorry for my disrespect."
- Gary makes a to-do list of undone tasks around the

house that are driving Lisa nuts. He takes an entire Saturday to take care of them, even though Lisa won't listen to his pleas to be more disciplined about the budget.

- Even though Tom fails to spend as much time with Lindsay as she wishes, she resolves to stop her tardiness so he doesn't have to wait for her in the car.

Is moving first always fair? No, of course not. There are times when it seems crystal clear which one should move first. But this isn't about "justice" or what is fair. It's about sucking it up and biting the bullet to stop the insanity of the Crazy Cycle and enjoy the motivation of the Energizing Cycle. As Hebrews 5 says, spiritual milk is for babies and solid food is for the mature ones who can recognize the right thing and then *just do it*.

First move anyone?

PRAYER: Thank the Lord for setting the example of always making the first move. Ask Him for the wisdom and strength to make the first move for each other in every situation, minor or major. Ask Him to help you stop the Crazy Cycle and stay on the Energizing Cycle, motivated by love and respect.

ACTION: This coming week (or month), practice being the mature one who makes the first move. Talk together about how it feels when one of you makes the first move to end a stalemate—and the Crazy Cycle. (For discussion questions, see page 252 in appendix A.)

CHAPTER 37

To Overcome the Past, Focus on the Prize

PHILIPPIANS 3:13–14:

Forgetting the past and looking forward to what lies ahead, I press on to reach the end of the race and receive the heavenly prize, for which God, through Christ Jesus, is calling us (NLT).

W e are living in a time and culture that is obsessed with winning. As one Indiana high school basketball coach put it, "Oh, Hoosier basketball fans love you— whether you win or tie."

He said it tongue in cheek, of course, but the point is well made. In any endeavor, losing is not really permitted. If you lose, especially if you get on a losing streak, people label you "loser." When I got a chance to speak to the New York Giants players and their coaches, wives, and girlfriends about Love & Respect, I was able to chat afterward with head coach Tom Coughlin, who shared with me about enduring some rough stretches before the Giants became Super Bowl champions. We discussed a lot of the problems he had faced: pressure from the press and being hounded by fanatical fans, especially during losing streaks. As we talked, he mentioned that in the NFL coaches are hired and fired like flies swatted on the wall. If you don't win, "So long!"

Thinking I might glean some wisdom to share with Love & Respect couples, I asked, "How do you deal with adversity?" His answer was immediate, spoken with conviction: "You keep your eye on the prize."

Tom lives by his "eye on the prize" credo and preaches it constantly to his players and assistant coaches. When pressure mounts and difficulties multiply, you focus on the big picture and ultimate goal. Tom became head coach of the Giants in 2004, and in a town like New York nothing will do but winning the Super Bowl. Despite being the target of withering criticism and cynicism, the Giants improved each year, kept making the playoffs, and finally, on February 3, 2008, the Super Bowl championship was theirs as they upset the heavily favored New England Patriots, 17–14.[1]

A nice sports story, you may be thinking, *but exactly what does it have to do with my marriage?* Quite a bit—maybe everything. You and your spouse are a team, and like any other team you have your wins and your losses. Sometimes adversity seems to hit from within and without, and you go on a losing streak. What then?

We have already looked at getting right back up if you fall (chapter 1) and having the courage to admit mistakes (chapter 6). But sometimes it helps to have some extra motivation to deal with setbacks, and we find it in today's key verse: Philippians 3:13–14. If anyone knew something about dealing with adversity, it was Paul the apostle. He was hounded by those who hated him, rejected when he preached Christ, and even stoned and left for dead, but he pressed on, with his eye on the prize. And what was the prize? Not a Super Bowl ring, but a crown of righteousness awarded at the judgment seat of Christ (2 Timothy 4:8).

In basketball-crazy Indiana, high school coaches may be loved only if they "win or tie," but because of your faith in Christ, you are loved, *win or lose.* You and your spouse can press on, knowing that something glorious awaits you if you persevere. No matter what form adversity takes, no matter what the setback might be, *do not see yourself as a loser.* Your race is not over. You have another day to run.

In a letter to the sports-happy Corinthians, Paul observes: "All athletes are disciplined in their training. They do it to win a prize that will fade away, but we do it for an eternal prize" (1 Corinthians 9:25 NLT). The question for every Love & Respect couple is, how important, really, is that eternal prize? When you fail to love or respect and the Crazy Cycle roars into action, what

> INSIGHT: Wins, losses, or ties, press on toward the prize!

will you do? Become your own worst critics, because this Love & Respect thing seems just too difficult? Not if you take the long view. Marriage is not a fifty-yard dash; it is part of the marathon all Christ followers run. As Paul says, forget the past with its setbacks and its losses, and press on. The prize is waiting.

PRAYER: Ask the Lord to help you overcome the pain of the past, real as it still may be, as you focus on heaven's prize. Ask Him for the courage and perseverance to keep your eye on the prize—His upward call in Christ Jesus. Thank the Father that He loves you— win, lose, or tie.

ACTION: Agree together that when setbacks occur, you will say to each other, "Forget yesterday's loss. Let's focus on today's opportunity, because of tomorrow's prize." (For discussion questions, see page 253 in appendix A.)

CHAPTER 38

Is My Response *Always* My Responsibility?

JOHN 8:31–32, 36:

"If you hold to my teaching, you are really my disciples. Then you will know the truth, and the truth will set you free. . . . [And] if the Son sets you free, you will be free indeed" (NIV).

I n the give and take of a Love & Respect marriage, which of these statements is true?

A. My response could be my responsibility.
B. My response could be my spouse's responsibility.
C. It depends on the situation; it could go either way.

The correct answer, of course, is "none of the above." When seeking to unconditionally love or respect your spouse, your response is *always* your responsibility. There is no wiggling off the hook with the phrase "could be." Oh, we all like to think there could be a way to avoid taking responsibility. I do at times. *Surely*, I tell myself, *there must be a reason why my less-than-loving response is really Sarah's responsibility*, but not so.

Let me put it this way. Sarah doesn't cause me to be the way I am; she reveals the way I am. When I am unloving toward Sarah, it's because I still have issues. I still have more growing up to do. When we spin on the Crazy Cycle, Sarah is not causing me to disobey God's command to love. That's my choice. The same holds true for you. Your spouse does not cause you to sin but reveals your choice to sin.

> INSIGHT: My response is *always* my responsibility.

For example, think about stepping on a rose. As you crush it, a lovely fragrance comes forth. Stepping on a skunk also discharges an odor. 'Nuff said. Did the pressure on the rose and skunk cause the resulting smell, or did it reveal the inner properties of the rose and skunk? In your marriage you need to realize your spouse doesn't cause you to be a rose or a skunk. You reveal your own "inner fragrance."

The idea that it's what's inside that counts may sound daunting, even intimidating. But as I thought it through, I realized that no one controls me. I am not a helpless victim. I have a choice between being a rose or a skunk. Having a choice is in itself very empowering and liberating, but the best part is that I do not have to make that choice alone. I have Jesus, and ultimately He makes all the difference. As today's verse teaches, the Son has set me free, and that makes me free indeed to take responsibility for how I react to Sarah in any situation.

I have many e-mails from people who agree. They apply their freedom in Christ daily, refusing to respond unlovingly or disrespectfully, even when tempted, as one lady put it, "to disappear him." And as one husband reported, "We both were the skunk, depending on the situation," but that's over, and things are getting better gradually because the phrase keeps echoing in his head: *my response is my responsibility.*

For the Love & Respect couple there is no more bailing out by saying, in so many words, "Well, honey, you know my response is really *your* responsibility. You made me put us on the Crazy Cycle." Instead, both of you know you have the power to act like adults and take responsibility to be loving and respectful. Why? When the Son sets you free, you are free indeed!

PRAYER: Thank the Lord that you know the Son and the Son has set you free to make the right choice, no matter what has been said or what has gone on. Thank Him also for the freedom to take personal responsibility. Ask Him to give you the grace and courage to deal with the many opportunities in every twenty-four-hour day to unconditionally love and respect each other. (Also pray about taking the Insight for this devotional along to work, church, and other settings. The Christian's response is *always* his or her responsibility!)

ACTION: This week, leave Post-it notes throughout the house, in the car, and at your workplace with this reminder: "My response is always my responsibility." At the end of the week (or another agreed-upon amount of time), talk together about the effect this has had on your interactions. (For discussion questions, see page 254 in appendix A.)

CHAPTER 39

LOOK! JUST OVER YOUR SPOUSE'S SHOULDER! IT'S JESUS!

MATTHEW 25:40:

"I tell you the truth, whatever you did for one of the least of these brothers of mine, you did for me" (NIV).

As we come to the last session of a Love & Respect conference, we close with the Rewarded Cycle—the very heart and soul of the Love & Respect Connection. And why is it the heart and soul? Because it teaches husbands and wives this all-important truth:

In the ultimate sense, your marriage has nothing to do with your spouse.

It has everything to do with your relationship to Jesus Christ.

The scriptural basis for this statement is Jesus' parable of the last judgment (Matthew 25:31–46). Those deemed righteous ask, "Lord, when did we see you hungry and feed you, or thirsty and give you something to drink? When did we see you a stranger and invite you in, or needing clothes and clothe you? When did we see you sick or in prison and go to visit you?" (vv. 37–39). The King answers the righteous and says, "I tell you the truth, whatever you did for one of the least of these brothers of mine, you did for me" (v. 40).

The audience quickly sees the application to them: *whatever I do for my spouse, I do for Christ as well.* A husband's unconditional love for his wife reveals his love for Christ. If love for her is missing, so is love for Christ. A wife's unconditional respect for her husband reveals her reverence for Christ. If respect for him is missing, so is reverence for Christ.

All of us must make the personal application. Jesus is saying, *Emerson, look at me. This isn't about Sarah. She may not deserve love—that's not the point. You show love to Sarah in order to show Me that you love me. Or, Sarah, look at me. This isn't about Emerson. Yes, he needs to change, but this is about you coming across respectfully as your way of showing your reverence for Me.*

> **INSIGHT:** To love or respect your spouse is to love and respect your Lord.

To seal this idea, I use one of the most memorable images of the entire conference. Whatever you do by way of love or respect, you do not do it primarily to get your marriage off the Crazy Cycle. Nor do you do it to get your spouse to meet your needs. Ultimately, to practice love or respect, especially in moments of tension or conflict, you look at your spouse and just over his or her shoulder you envision Jesus Christ, standing there looking at you, saying, *Truly, as you have done it to your spouse, you have done it unto Me!*

As I tell the crowd, "When I see Jesus back there behind Sarah, it's as if I hear Him saying, *Emerson, this isn't about Sarah, this is about you and Me. Yes, I see her finger in your face as she scolds you for being unloving. Yes, I agree she could be more respectful. So what will you do? Just walk away, or look beyond her to Me because, as a man of honor, you will do the loving thing as unto Me?*"

I get letter after letter about the Christ-over-the-shoulder image. Here's an example: "If I see Jesus looking at me over my husband's shoulder, then I'm bound to treat my husband with the respect due to him out of my love and reverence for Jesus. I do believe that was the single brightest lightbulb flash for me!"

To realize you are doing your marriage as unto Christ is revolutionizing—and sobering. The image of Christ standing there, just beyond your spouse's shoulder *as part of every conversation,* is a reminder that you will be standing before Him at the final judgment. As you envision Him, you will more fully understand that your marriage is really a tool and a test to deepen and demonstrate your love and your reverence for your Lord. You will grasp the power of the Rewarded Cycle:

His love blesses regardless of her respect.
Her respect blesses regardless of his love.

PRAYER: Thank the Lord for being the "seen" guest in every conversation you have together. Pray for the strength and wisdom to always envision Him at the center of your marriage, especially in moments of tension or conflict.

ACTION: As you talk together, each of you can practice seeing Christ over each other's shoulder. Talk about how this feels. What is the Lord telling you? (For discussion questions, see page 255 in appendix A.)

CHAPTER 40

If Only We Didn't Have Money Problems

PHILIPPIANS 4:19:

*And my God will supply all your needs according to His
riches in glory in Christ Jesus.*

Emerson, we agree with the Love & Respect message, but
we have money problems. We'd have a really great marriage if we didn't have these financial pressures."

I receive many e-mails just like this, from couples who believe
lack of money is the root of their marital problems. I understand
why they say that. Financial problems can cause tremendous
pressures and frustrations. In fact, many marriage experts claim
that money mismanagement is the main source of marital discord. Yes, money problems are very real, but they are not the root
reason that friendship and intimacy fade as she feels unloved and
he feels disrespected. Money squabbles don't undermine love and
respect; they simply reveal unloving and disrespectful attitudes,
which are the real reason why a marriage can start to wobble on
the Crazy Cycle.

During a heated discussion about money, it is all too easy to appear hostile, sarcastic, or even contemptuous. It may be for only a few seconds, but it is enough to deflate the spirit of your spouse. Mark it down: money problems simply reveal what is in our hearts, how mature or immature we really are. Ouch! That hurts, I know, but it can be true of any of us.

Think of a toddler who throws himself kicking on the floor when he realizes he cannot have what he wants at the store. Being deprived of what he wants does not cause his temper tantrums; it simply reveals his immaturity. But what about us when we are deprived of what we want? Does being an adult guarantee that we will not overreact when we find ourselves in a financial situation contrary to our liking?

Some spouses think, *if we just had more money, then we'd be happy.* How different, really, is this reasoning from that of a little kid, lying there kicking on the floor, thinking, *if I can just get Mom to buy me that piece of candy, then I will be happy?*

INSIGHT: The Lord will provide for all our needs; we may have to wait for our wants.

Immaturity on someone's part may or may not be at least part of any couple's money problems. But what exactly *do* you do when once again there is more month than money and you find tempers are about to flare? All kinds of money problems can suddenly descend. The question is, will a couple confront these problems together, showing each other love and respect, or will they turn away from each other and even the Lord because of anger and frustration?

When money problems close in, we have our best opportunity to deepen our maturity. The struggle to deal with money will remain real, but how glorious to wade through this quag-mire as a team and be confident in God to lead us out of the predicament. The choice is always ours. Ultimately, financial needs should cause two people to turn to Christ for His supply, and what a glorious promise in today's key verse! God will sup-ply our needs, but He wants us to be able to tell the difference between our needs and our wants.

Suppose, for example, you need transportation to work, and you have just enough cash to pay for a pre-owned vehicle with decent miles that has been well cared for. But at the last second, you spot a practically new convertible in mint condition. Of course, it costs a lot more, but you manage to finance it and drive off the lot feeling you got what you always wanted. Yes, you did. But in six months the big payments are putting you under severe financial stress. What happened to that promise in Philippians 4:19? It is still there. He nicely provided for your need with that older vehicle, but you wanted that convertible and you wound up with money problems.

King Solomon, who knew quite a bit about making poor decisions, said, "The stupidity of a person turns his life upside down, and his heart rages against the LORD" (Proverbs 19:3 GW). Raging against the Lord for not providing enough for our wants is childish. Instead, we can put James 1:5 into action. Does it say God will drop the money into our laps? No, but it does promise the wisdom to budget carefully and find the Lord providing a way when there seems to be no way. As He parted the Red Sea for Moses, the Lord can part our "seas of red"—if we let Him!

PRAYER: Thank the Lord for any money problems you may have at the moment, because they give you the opportunity to trust Him more. Ask Him to supply your needs, as He shows you what to do to meet your financial obligations.

ACTION: Sort out together your needs and your wants. Be honest with each other, but always with love and respect. If your financial challenges are severe, you may want to consider seeing a skilled Christian counselor—see appendix D (page 289) for counseling resources. (For discussion questions, see page 257 in appendix A.)

CHAPTER 41

Your Spouse Has Needs Only You Can Fill

PHILIPPIANS 2:4–5:

Don't be concerned only about your own interests, but also be concerned about the interests of others. Have the same attitude that Christ Jesus had (GW).

You may have heard more than one sermon on today's key verse, usually applied to life in the church with fellow believers. But have you thought about how it applies to your marriage? What better place not to be concerned with only your own agenda but to be at least equally concerned about your spouse's interests, concerns, hopes, and dreams. Why? What should be your incentive? Love and respect? Yes, but even more fundamental is that you "have the same attitude that Christ Jesus had" (Philippians 2:5).

Of course, this means putting your own needs aside, at least for the moment. It means sacrificing for the sake of the one you decided to spend your life with. Sarah is a great example of doing just that. It is not Sarah's first choice to endure the stress of getting us to the airport and then take another long ride to a faraway city for the next L&R conference. But Sarah puts her interests aside for the sake of the ministry, for which I am far more thankful than I can express on paper or even in person. To say, "She is invaluable," would be a gross understatement.

And what about Emerson? What is his sacrifice? My obvious main interests in life are studying, writing, and preparing material. One of Sarah's interests (perhaps it is her main interest) is engaging in the well-documented Pinkie pastime of talking, particularly with me. Over the years I have learned to put aside my studying and writing to hear her concerns several times a week, if not daily.

Sarah will tell you that I have truly given of myself to allow her to talk. I have not shut down, saying, "I am the way I am. Deal with it!" (I admit I have had the thought a few times, but God is good, and He has protected me from myself, not to mention my sweet little wife.)

INSIGHT: Self-interest should never come ahead of your spouse's interests.

The point of today's key verse is clear: don't just be concerned about your own agenda; think about the interests of others—especially your spouse (see Philippians 2:4). So far, so good, but is there some motivation that would help us do this, besides the fear of feeling guilty if we don't come through? We find a very big clue in verse 5: "Have the same attitude that Christ Jesus had." As the rest of what is called the "kenosis passage" points out, Jesus "emptied himself," putting aside His deity to live among us and meet our deepest need—salvation from our sin (see Philippians 2:6–11).

As you and your spouse seek to imitate your Savior and Lord within marriage, you quickly learn that you both have needs only the other can meet. Could that mean functioning outside your comfort zone and even feeling inadequate? Possibly, but your incentive is that your spouse needs you, no one else. That is not an imposition, it's a compliment worthy of praise to the heavenly Father, because such moments allow you to imitate Jesus and thereby honor Him. Such moments chip away your un-Christlike features as you "let the Spirit renew your thoughts and attitudes" (Ephesians 4:23 NLT).

So the next time you have an opportunity to look to the needs or concerns of your spouse when it is, quite frankly, inconvenient or even a bit painful for you, think about how your new attitude in Christ is helping sand off the rough edges of selfishness. Your spouse has a need only you can fill. Instead of bringing up a lot of reasons why you can't do it, or the things your spouse might do instead, see the situation for what it is. Say to yourself, or even aloud, "Thanks, honey, thanks for the compliment!"

PRAYER: Thank the Lord for His invitation to have the same attitude that Christ Jesus had, and for the ways He helps sand away the rough edges of self-interest as you both have opportunities to meet each other's needs for love and respect. Ask Him for the wisdom and humility to always see your spouse's needs as a compliment, not a cause for your complaints. (Also look outside the family, to work, church, and other situations where you can put the needs of others ahead of your own and have your actions come full-circle in various ways.)

ACTION: During the coming week, practice responding to each other's requests and needs by saying, "Thanks for the compliment." As a reminder to do this, put Post-it notes in strategic places saying, "Have the same attitude that Christ Jesus had." (For discussion questions, see page 258 in appendix A.)

But Is Your Spouse
Supposed to Meet *All*
Your Needs?

HEBREWS 4:16:

*Let us then approach the throne of grace with
confidence, so that we may receive mercy and find grace
to help us in our time of need (NIV).*

G etting married reveals, usually sooner than later, an incontestable fact: your spouse cannot possibly meet all your needs and desires. Many couples start out thinking that marriage will fulfill all their needs—emotional, physical, even spiritual. And then they spend years on the Crazy Cycle to one degree or another, because she thinks he should meet all her needs for love and he thinks she should meet all his needs for respect.

Sarah and I did this for a while until we both realized that thinking your spouse can meet all your needs is a dead end. So we settled the "meet all my needs" issue quite a while ago. We both know we are called to love and respect each other, and that we should put each other's needs ahead of our own (see chapter 41). But meet them *all*? It will never happen, because we are human. To say your spouse can meet all your needs, or even most of your needs, is futile because your spouse is not God.

In every marriage there are times when someone's needs are overlooked, and it becomes apparent that certain needs are just not going to be met completely by the person you married. Remember the 80:20 ratio regarding troubles that we talked about in chapter 5? It applies to needs as well. At least 20 percent of the time, quite likely even more, your spouse will not meet all your needs to your complete satisfaction. Moments like these can be wake-up calls asking both of you to realize that your deepest contentment and peace are in Christ, not in each other.

For example, a husband tries to listen attentively to his wife and meet her need for empathy and understanding, but he does not show the amount of empathy and understanding she desires. Truth be told, he could never show enough, hard as he might try. Should she be angry and reject him as unloving? Of course not; instead, this is the perfect time to turn to the Lord and entrust her need to Him.

Or suppose a wife tries to respond to her husband sexually, but she does not show as much interest and passion as he desires. He can feel rejected and disrespected, or he can look to the Lord for strength and patience.

Granted, turning to the Lord with your need when your spouse fails to meet it completely (or even not at all) takes the maturity to realize that difficulties and disappointments are not exceptions; they are quite often the rule. The good news is in Hebrews 4:16, which tells us to approach the Lord with confidence. He is ready to show us mercy and grace in our time of need, no matter what it is. God loves to see us bring our needs and weaknesses to Him. When we are weak, He is strong (2 Corinthians 12:9–10).

What can happen? One husband said, "I had to give my wife into God's hands . . . trust Him completely and surrender everything to Him. I had to look at myself and ask God to transform me into the man and husband He wanted me to be. I had to place my hope in Him!"

One wife realized that she had mistakenly believed that if her husband would just love her, her pain would be gone. And then she saw in the Scriptures that God alone should be her heart's desire: "God should be the one thing I seek. Everything else I desire should be such a distant second that even if I don't get my other desires, my love for God and His love for me satisfy my deepest longing for Him because I have what I really desire the most."

> INSIGHT: Your spouse may meet many of your needs, but your deepest dependency should be on your Lord.

This lady gets it and so must we. As strong and powerful as marriage bonds can become, our deepest dependency must be on the Lord, not another human being. As Psalm 73:25–26 puts it, we have no one in heaven but Him, and we should desire Him more than anything on earth. He and He alone is the ultimate strength for our hearts. He is ours forever!

PRAYER: Thank the Lord for imperfections (unmet desires) in your marriage because they drive you to ultimately depend on Him. Ask Him to help you open yourselves to the peace and contentment that only His presence can provide.

ACTION: Each of you could take time this week to assess how much you depend on each other. Can you see the line between healthy dependency on his love and her respect, and asking too much of each other? Then come together to compare notes and talk about "needing each other" but ultimately depending on the Lord. (For discussion questions, see page 259 in appendix A.)

CHAPTER 43

YOUR CHILDREN ARE WATCHING

DEUTERONOMY 11:18–19:

"Fix these words of mine in your hearts ... Teach them to your children, talking about them when you sit at home" (NIV).

I n Sunday school little Billy was asked, "What is faith?" He replied, "Faith is believing something that you know isn't true." This oft-quoted joke may make us smile, but if little Billy holds on to that idea, he'll walk away from the faith and that will not be funny.

What's the best way to encourage a child in the faith? Scripture makes it plain that Mom and Dad play the most vital role. When parents genuinely trust and follow the Lord and His ways, their faith spills over onto the children. That's what today's key verse is talking about. Moses is speaking, but the words are the Lord's as He spells out how the Israelites are to live and raise their families. First they are to fix God's words in their own hearts, then teach them to their children (Deuteronomy 11:18-19). Then and now, the challenge for parents has been the same:

How can we teach our kids and really transmit
our faith so they can make it their own?

As helpful as Sunday school and other church activities are,
your children learn a lot more just by watching you and your
spouse, not only as parents but as husband and wife. Do they
observe you treating each other with love and respect? What do
they see and hear that says loud and clear Mom and Dad love
God and each other? Here are a few questions to consider:

- Do our children see us praying together at times other
  than before meals? Do they hear us talking about
  depending on Christ to give strength and wisdom for
  what we should do about whatever is facing our family?
- Do our children learn from us during teachable moments
  that happen naturally? (For example, you could casually
  share with them what you are learning from these
  devotionals. They might be more interested than you
  think.)
- Do our children ever see any physical affection between
  us—a loving hug, kiss, pat, or squeeze? Can they see
  evidence that we really *like* each other?
- Do our children see us facing challenging times with
  a measure of peace and contentment instead of anger
  and worry? (When you squeeze an orange, orange juice
  comes out. When life squeezes you, does Jesus come
  out?)

These are just a few considerations; you can think of many
more that fit your family and the ages of your children. Your
goal is not to run a Sunday school class at home but to live

with your children in such a way that you infect them with the "real disease." You are trying to "sneeze faith" and hope you are contagious. Obviously, there are no guarantees that children will follow the faith of their parents. Each child makes his or her own choices and some choose to disobey (Romans 1:30; 2 Timothy 3:2). As a parent, your job is to live your faith before your children as genuinely and honestly as you can and leave the rest to God. Here are two more questions to ask yourselves from time to time:

- In our marriage, is there real love and respect?
- Do our kids see us as the "real deal" when it comes to our faith?

If you were to ask your children, "Do Mom and Dad love and respect each other?," how would they answer? And if you asked them, "Whom do Mom and Dad trust and follow the most in their lives?," what would be their reply?

These are hard, demanding questions that can make a parent sometimes think, *What's the use? The odds are against me.* But then you remember that you are not in this parenting thing alone. You know that you can greatly increase the odds that your children will love and reverence Christ when you do. It's as simple . . . and hard . . . as

> **INSIGHT:** Your hunger for God can create an appetite in your children.

that. Welcome the fact that your marriage has an audience. Your children are watching. Will they see the real deal?

PRAYER: Thank the Lord for your children, acknowledging that they are gifts from Him. Ask Him for the strength and faith to teach your children how to trust and obey as they watch you trust and obey. Ask Him to increase your hunger for His Word and create a hunger in your children as well.

ACTION: This week, as the time seems right, ask your children, "Who do Mom and Dad trust and follow the most in life?" And, if they are old enough to understand your commitment to love and respect, ask them how they think you are doing. (For discussion questions, see page 260 in appendix A.)

CHAPTER 44

I Am *Not* Being Defensive!

PROVERBS 18:19:

An offended friend is harder to win back than a fortified city.
Arguments separate friends like a gate locked with iron bars (NLT).

Why is it sometimes so easy to offend each other without even trying? I know with Sarah and me, either one of us can get defensive when the other is pointing out something that needs changing. No matter how tactfully the suggestion is made, it is quite natural to get a bit touchy. When you feel slightly attacked—just a bit unloved or disrespected—it is easy to put up your defenses and then, sad to say, counterattack.

To put it in terms I use when teaching, feeling unloved, a wife gets *defensive* and acts *offensively* without respect. Feeling disrespected, a husband gets *defensive* and acts *offensively* without love.

To illustrate how this works, here is an example of how I can be defensive and quickly switch to being offensive. Sarah might address something in my life that I need to be more sensitive to, such as e-mailing people back more quickly. Because I believe

I am trying my best to keep up with everything, I feel a little disrespected. Rationally, my head tells me she has no intention of being disrespectful, but it is just too easy to react at an emotional level. So I get defensive, and that easily leads to my counterattack: "Well, the other day, you fell asleep while our friend Ray was sharing his heart with us about his new job. How sensitive was that?"

Of course, I should not have been so childish, but that twinge of defensiveness had me wanting to prove I was not so bad after all. I should have let it go and said I would try to get to the e-mails as soon as I could. Instead, I allowed my feelings to convince me I was being disrespected, and I chose to turn the situation back on Sarah and lash out without love.

Sarah's countenance fell. I felt justified. We both pulled back and did not talk for over an hour as the Crazy Cycle hummed quietly along. Today's scripture passage describes the situation perfectly. Sarah was offended; her fortifications were up and iron bars were locking the gate.

> **INSIGHT:** When you get defensive, you go on the offensive—and both of you can go on the Crazy Cycle.

As the minutes ticked by, I had twinges of conscience. Finally, I realized what I had done to defend my pride, and from there it was a no-brainer, even for me. When we finally resumed our conversation, Sarah asked, "Why do you say things like that when I am trying to help you?" As we discussed the situation, I finally stepped up and said what I should have said an hour before: "I'm sorry. I was really unloving. Will you forgive me?"

Fortunately, Sarah put her hurt feelings aside and accepted my apology. But as the Crazy Cycle ground to a halt, she did add (respectfully, of course), "It would have been nice if you had apologized sooner, and it would also be nice if you wouldn't get so defensive when I am trying to help you." (At this point, I am happy to report that I did *not* get defensive!)

PRAYER: Ask the Lord for forgiveness for times of defensiveness that lead to offensive counterattacks and the Crazy Cycle. Ask Him to work His will in your marriage by making both of you more mature and humble enough to treat each other with love and respect. (Is anything happening at work or at church that is making you defensive? Pray about this too. We bring home problems from wherever we spend our time.)

ACTION: Resolve that when your spouse tells you something about yourself that you don't like, you will *not* say, "Well, you do the same." Instead, you will make an effort to bite your tongue and not be defensive. (For discussion questions, see page 262 in appendix A.)

CHAPTER 45

How Positive Are You with Each Other?

PHILIPPIANS 4:8:

Finally, my brothers and sisters, always think about what is true.
Think about what is noble, right and pure. Think about what is
lovely and worthy of respect. If anything is excellent or worthy of
praise, think about those kinds of things (NIRV).

On a scale of 1 to 10, how positive are you with your spouse?

One of the most positive e-mails I ever received on this question came from a wife who wrote, "I felt God saying to me, *I want you to imagine you are a giant highlighter, and I want you to highlight all the things that are honorable and true about your husband. Think on these things. See your husband through My eyes.* I sat up in bed and started writing—filling pages with beautiful things I wanted to respect my husband for. I fell in love with him all over that night."

When I e-mailed her to ask permission to quote her, she

commented that she loves to highlight key thoughts in books, and she believes God gave her the highlighter idea as a way to honor and respect her husband. She added that God also brought Philippians 4:8–9 to mind, a passage she calls "His gift to me."

Philippians 4:8 is God's gift to all married couples. Read it right now, slowly and carefully. When Paul speaks of what is true, noble, right, pure, lovely, and worthy of respect, he is saying that *through dependence on God, we can control what we think.* We can put the negative out of our minds by setting our thoughts on the good—the positive.[1]

And don't miss verse 9. Paul invites us to put into practice what we have learned from him. Focusing on the positive is a discipline. It does not come naturally, but it can be done. It's up to us. It is our choice.

> INSIGHT: Accentuate the positive and eliminate the negative, with lots of love and respect in between.

True, some people are more positive by nature, while others are more likely to see the glass half empty. A friend told me of how his wife, positive by nature, would get angry when he said anything negative (what he called "being realistic"). When she became terminally ill for a long period of time, he made a deliberate effort to stay positive in words and actions right up to the moment she died in his arms. His story tells me that even if your temperament is bent toward the melancholy and pessimistic, you can choose to dwell on the noble and positive, *if you want to.*

How are you coming across in your marriage—negative or positive? I heard the story of a pro football player who got a long-overdue physical exam and was told that some of his test results would take over a week. During this time his wife was challenged in a woman's Bible study to be positive, respectful, and friendly with her husband, so she tried to do just that. After several days of being treated in this positive and friendly manner, the husband smelled a rat. This was not like his wife at all. "Okay, tell me," he said. "The doctor talked to you and told you I have a terminal illness. I am going to die, right?" He had concluded that she was being nice because he wouldn't be around much longer![2]

As we discussed this story, Sarah commented, "I don't think women realize how unfriendly they can become in the home. One of the greatest ways we can honor and respect our husbands is to continue to be the friend that we were when we first met." Sarah is right. Ironically, it is all too easy for stress, pressure, a shortage of money, and so on to cause us to be brusque, short-tempered, and less than friendly with the one we say we love.

So, coming back to my original question, on a scale of 1 to 10, how positive am I with my spouse? I can think of little things Sarah does that bug me (like clearing her throat) and she can think of things I do that bug her (like leaving wet towels lying around). Or we can think of things we like about each other. I can think of what is lovely and lovable in her; she can think of what is worthy of respect in me. It is always our choice. It is always your choice too. *Think about it!*

PRAYER: Thank the Lord for Paul's reminder list in Philippians 4:8. Ask Him for the discipline to apply this list to each other as you seek to always see your marriage glass half full and more.

ACTION: Try being "giant highlighters" this week and write down lists of what is true, noble, right, pure, lovely, and worthy of respect about each other. Then talk about what you see in each other that is excellent and praiseworthy. When negative things come up (and they will), deal with them together in a positive way. (For discussion questions, see page 263 in appendix A.)

CHAPTER 46

DO YOU EVER PLAY THE BLAME GAME?

GENESIS 3:12:

The man replied, "It was the woman you gave me who gave me the fruit, and I ate it" (NLT).

L et's have a little fun with a legendary nursery rhyme, to help us think about a widespread habit that can undermine any marriage:

Humpty Dumpty sat on a wall.
Humpty Dumpty had a great fall.
Humpty Dumpty started to bawl:
"I was pushed!"

This probably isn't the way you remember the saga of Humpty. The original rhyme had something about all the king's horses and all the king's men, and so forth. But in my revised version I would like to consider the possibility that Humpty was not pushed but simply fell off due to his own carelessness and immediately started to blame somebody else.

Did Humpty have a wife? There is no way to know for sure, but if he did, she might have been his logical suspect. Ever since the Fall, husbands and wives have been skilled in placing blame. Adam blamed Eve, Eve blamed the serpent, and the rest is the history of the human race. (Someone once pointed out to me that the serpent had no one to blame; he didn't have a leg to stand on.)

If you think about it, the first sin after the "Big Sin" was blame placing, and it has become the name of the game for human beings, especially married ones. Passing the buck! It seems to come so naturally. Why are we so quick and inventive at imputing guilt? I think it has something to do with being afraid to take total responsibility. We have already looked at the concept that one's response is one's responsibility (see chapter 38). And while we may agree with this noble idea in principle, we hold just a bit of reservation about taking *all* the blame. After all, whatever goes on does not take place in a vacuum. And so Blue explains, "Her disrespect goaded me into being unloving." And Pink quickly points out, "He is so unloving; how can I respect him?"

> INSIGHT: When you play the blame game, your marriage never wins. Pass not the buck!

So what happens when we play this sorry game? I can still hear Sarah's voice from early in our marriage. "It's always me. I'm always to blame." Trying to make Sarah the scapegoat didn't work back then, and it doesn't work now, with her or with God. He has been hearing blame-placing excuses since Adam let Him know that it was actually His fault that he had sinned! "It was the woman you gave me who brought me the fruit, and I ate it" (Genesis 3:12). How like Adam I can be at times (perhaps you can identify). I try to justify myself by blaming the woman I love for my own indiscretions and transgressions, when I know full well that my Lord and Savior is the only One who can justify any of us (see Romans 3:24).

In our Love & Respect travels, Sarah and I got to know LPGA golfer Barb Whitehead, a Christ follower who shared some excellent insights on placing blame where it belongs:

> It truly does come down to my choice in how I treat Trent, no matter what he says to me. In the end I have to answer to the Lord about what I did with the man God gave me. With that choice comes freedom because I know I am solely responsible. I think taking that responsibility comes from my former vocation of golf. I had no one else to blame for the bad shot or missed putt but myself. That can seem like pressure, but for me it was really freeing. I see my response to Trent the same way. I have the freedom to respond to him in a Christlike manner, so always, it's my choice.[1]

Barb's insights make perfect sense, whether you're hovering over a five-footer for par, or deciding if what you are about to say will be loving or respectful. In every situation, don't blame your spouse; instead, turn to Christ for the power to respond the way you should.

PRAYER: Thank the Lord that He has set the example for not placing blame, by sending Christ to take the blame for all of us. Ask Him for the wisdom and courage not to pass the buck, but to take responsibility for your actions instead of blaming others.

ACTION: Throughout the coming week, try keeping track of how often you are tempted to blame your spouse for something when you were really at fault, fully or partially. Talk together about what you are learning about placing blame where it belongs. (For discussion questions, see page 264 in appendix A.)

CHAPTER 47

GROUPTHINK CAN BE TOXIC TO YOUR MARRIAGE

PROVERBS 13:20:

Anyone who walks with wise people grows wise. But a companion of foolish people suffers harm (NIRV).

E ver hear of *groupthink*? It is a typical practice among the Pink gender (but men do it, too, in their own Blue way). Picture a group of gals who get together regularly for coffee or lunch. As often as not, the subject of husbands comes up and they compare notes on what their husbands do to drive them a little crazy. As they talk, the picture that gets painted ranges from unfavorable to downright negative.

If a wife in the group raises a voice of dissent by pointing out that "men are not wrong, just different," she is pressured to change her "erroneous perspective," or she is kindly dismissed as a lucky exception. If there are other wives present who really agree with the dissenter, they are likely to remain quiet, thinking that solidarity in the group takes precedence over honest discussion of the facts.

Husbands can also be guilty of groupthink by reducing women to one-sentence descriptions, such as "Women, you can't live with them, but you can't live without them," or "Women are emotional and unreasonable," or "Oh my, the drama!" Yes, there can be husbands who don't use these phrases, but they usually stay silent because they don't want to appear henpecked or unmanly.

And let us not forget TV, films, and other media, which often spew forth groupthink of one kind or another, putting down husbands as simpleminded oafs, or labeling women as overdramatic basket cases, just to get laughs.

Warning: groupthink can be toxic to your marriage and must be countered with "Godthink." By buying into the typical stereotypes about what is wrong with men or women, wives are much more likely to see their husbands only through their Pink sunglasses, and husbands will see their wives only through their Blue ones. This is a surefire way to feed the Crazy Cycle.

> INSIGHT: Godthink builds love and respect in your marriage; groupthink tears it down.

For example, when a wife reacts negatively because she is feeling unloved, a groupthink-influenced husband could easily dismiss her reaction as "just being overdramatic again," instead of looking more deeply into her heart to try to understand her, which is what God commands. Result: she will feel even more unloved!

Or when a husband reacts negatively because he is feeling disrespected, a groupthink-influenced wife could just write him off as childish, narcissistic, chauvinistic, or even abusive, instead of seeking God's help to dig beneath the surface to discover what is wrong. Result: he will feel even more disrespected!

In either case, groupthink wins the day, your marriage loses, and around and around the Crazy Cycle can spin. To paraphrase today's scripture verse: foolish people succumb to groupthink. Wise people use Godthink and stop the Crazy Cycle cold!

PRAYER: Ask the Lord for the strength and courage to refuse to go along with groupthinkers, even those who are friends or family. Thank Him for seeing the two of you as two people in need of a little love and respect, and ask for the wisdom to see each other as He does.

ACTION: Refuse to take part in groupthink of any kind, especially when bashing the opposite sex takes over. To be wise in the ways of male and female, hang out with people who appreciate and understand the differences between husbands and wives. (For discussion questions, see page 265 in appendix A.)

CHAPTER 48

DO YOU KNOW HOW
TO FIGHT FAIR?

2 CORINTHIANS 10:3:

The world is unprincipled. It's dog-eat-dog out there! The world doesn't fight fair. But we don't live or fight our battles that way—never have and never will (MSG).

O n a bright Sunday morning in Orlando, Florida, I spoke to five NFL head coaches and their wives on the topic of Love & Respect. I covered the Crazy Cycle and how a wife needs love and a husband needs respect, then we had a short break. While I chatted with some of the coaches, one of them exclaimed, "This is fascinating. We just got in a fight on the way here in the car on this very issue. I was saying, 'I need you to respect me!' She was saying, 'I need you to love me!'"

The irony of it all had struck him, but he was also encouraged to discover that lack of love and respect is the root issue of many "fights." By the time the mini-seminar was over, he and his wife had some tools to deal with disagreements. They were helped by their new understanding that almost all couples argue and fight. Trouble is, most couples have never learned how to do it productively.

I have counseled thousands of couples, and typically the wife is highly verbal, able to shred her husband's arguments with ease. Then he finally blows and winds up stonewalling her because he doesn't know what else to do. For example, one husband reports, "A week ago we got into another one of our Crazy Cycles. She calls them discussions; I call them fights. I don't even remember what it was over. She said her piece, I got silent, she got more vocal, and I continued to withdraw until I blew up and stormed out of the house. Every 'discussion' goes that way."

> INSIGHT: Fight like a loving man and a respectful woman: *fight fair.*

No wonder many couples tell me, "We are tired of fighting." I reply that they are on the right track; what they must try is disagreeing more agreeably, or when a fight breaks out, "fighting fair." In other words, they should fight like Christ followers, not with the dog-eat-dog carnal tactics Paul mentions in our key verse.

True, Paul is speaking primarily of people in the Corinthian church who were employing unprincipled methods because they disagreed with him, but the same standards for fighting fair apply to believers who are trying to build a godly, biblical marriage. Paul is saying that those who claim to follow Christ can argue (or fight) in one of two ways: "in the flesh," with manipulation, anger, jealousy, sarcasm, and harshness; or fairly, with civility, courtesy, gentleness, tact, and a willingness to honor opinions different from theirs.

Obviously, the civil approach calls us to depend on Christ's might and wisdom, which is Paul's point and is something we can all apply. You and your spouse may need no help with learning to argue or fight fair, but just in case, here is my suggestion. The next time you get into a husband-wife "discussion," just pray in your heart: *Lord, give me Your understanding right now and work in me with Your power. I need Your help and strength. I don't want to fight according to my "flesh"—that gets me nowhere. Help me argue my point with love or respect.*

Learning to fight fair is not easy for many of us, but it's worth it. One wife testifies, "It was nice to talk about what happened. It was nice to tell my husband that even though I am mad, I still respect him as a man and a husband. I told him to let me know when I am showing disrespect so I can stop because I don't even realize that I am doing it. When I said that, I saw something in him change."

Of course, it isn't always that rosy. Some couples have to learn to agree to disagree, at least some of the time. The important thing is to keep a positive attitude. I like the way one spouse puts it: "We don't always agree. However, it comes out a lot more respectful and a lot more loving!"

PRAYER: Thank God that He never promised you would not disagree, argue, or even fight, but that He has given you the strength to deal with your differences in the power of His Spirit. Ask Him for the wisdom and humility to disagree agreeably—with love and respect.

ACTION: The next time you disagree, argue, or fight, stop and think: *Am I being fair? Friendly? Civil? Gentle? Godly?* Talk together about how to develop code words or phrases to use when fighting fair. (For discussion ideas and more tips for fighting fair, see page 266 in appendix A.)

CHAPTER 49

Your Words Reveal Your Heart

JAMES 3:2:

Indeed, we all make many mistakes. For if we could control our tongues, we would be perfect and could also control ourselves in every other way (NLT).

I t is one thing to pledge love and respect to one another; it is another to bring it off daily, especially through what we say. For example, if Sarah is talking with me about something and I reply with an absentminded "uh-huh" as my attention wanders to the TV screen or the newspaper, she might dismiss it the first time, thinking anyone can be distracted. But if I continue to sneak glances at the TV screen or the paper while she is giving me her report for the day, she could easily start to feel unloved. She might try to laugh it off, saying, "Oh, that's just the way he is—always thinking about something," but inside, her "heart may be in pain" (Proverbs 14:13).

If I tell Sarah I love her but pay little attention as she talks to me, she can quickly wonder how much I really mean it. I need to communicate my love, with words, yes, but also with my attention. Grunts, uh-huhs, and um-hums do not cut it. She doesn't need a page of original romantic poetry daily; she just wants my eye contact and focused listening. There are many ways to say "I love you," and Sarah quickly detects when it comes from my heart.

And of course, the reverse is also true. Suppose I try to tell Sarah how satisfying it was to help someone with a marital problem that day on the phone or in an e-mail. If she just says, "Yes, well, that's great, honey. What do you want for dinner tonight?" I could begin thinking that she does not value my work all that much. Or if I invite her to watch a special feature on the evening news and she says, "You go ahead—I need to call some friends," it would be a small jump for me to start wondering if she really has much respect for me in her heart. There are many ways to communicate respect, and I can quickly tell when it is genuine and from Sarah's heart.

Granted, you might be thinking, *Wait a minute, just because I slip up, get distracted, or use careless words doesn't mean I have no love or respect in my heart. Nobody speaks perfectly all the time. Nobody always says just the right thing every moment of the day.* That's a good point, but I am talking about patterns and habits. Sarah and I admit that neither of us speaks perfectly all the time. As today's verse puts it, we all make mistakes, often with our tongues, but what is the solution? If we can control our tongues, we control ourselves. We realize that if we are interested in living out our love and respect, we must

> INSIGHT: Carefully measured words of love and respect reach from the head to the heart.

do all we can to measure our words carefully. We won't bat a thousand and talk perfectly every time, *but we can ask God to help us talk less imperfectly.*

Does that sound like aiming too low? We don't think so. As we measure our words and ask God for the wisdom to talk less imperfectly, we listen better to the love and respect that flows from our hearts to each other.

PRAYER: Thank the Lord for the many opportunities you both have each day to communicate love and respect. Ask Him for the wisdom to measure your words carefully as you speak love and respect from the heart.

ACTION: This week, try making a special effort to communicate your love and respect to each other with measured words and focused attention. At the end of the week, make time to talk together about what you have learned and how you can continue the practice. (For discussion questions, see page 268 in appendix A.)

CHAPTER 50

WHY WE ALL NEED RESPECT

1 PETER 3:1–2:

*In the same way, you wives, be submissive to your own
husbands . . . as they observe your chaste and respectful behavior.*

1 PETER 3:7:

*Husbands, in the same way be considerate as you live with your
wives, and treat them with respect (NIV).*

Anyone who has read *Love & Respect* knows that I stress
giving husbands respect, not because they deserve it, but
because they need it desperately. So desperately, in fact,
that once the typical husband starts hearing words of respect
from his wife, he often starts loving her as she most desires to
be loved.

As couples have made the Love & Respect Connection, thousands of marriages have been saved, strengthened, and enriched.
Couples understand that the Beatles were wrong when they
sang, "All You Need Is Love." Yes, love may "make the world

go 'round," but love is *not* sufficient to make a marriage work. Respect has been the missing element, especially for husbands, and once couples make the L&R Connection, wonderful things begin to happen.

Interestingly enough, however, as we have begun surveying couples with a standardized questionnaire before and after Love & Respect conferences, we have learned that wives and husbands are making it a point to *tell each other*, "I respect you." *Both spouses* seem to want and need respect. Of course, love is still important, even vital, for wives, but I keep hearing them also say, "How can I get him to respect me? I feel I receive a lot of love from him, but I also need respect and appreciation."

The apostle Peter definitely agrees. In 1 Peter 3:1–7, his powerful passage on intimacy in marriage, he says nothing about love. Instead he focuses on the need for wives to show husbands "chaste and respectful behavior" (v. 2) and for husbands to be considerate of their wives, treating them with honor and respect (see v. 7).

Why didn't Peter preach love in marriage? Married himself, Peter knew that overromantic notions associated with "real love" can mislead and disillusion a couple when the daily duties, troubles, and concerns of marriage descend in full force. A Jew, reared in the Old Testament, Peter had often read the steamy passages from Song of Solomon, but he also knew that Solomon and his Shulammite beauty

> INSIGHT: Love fires a marriage; respect keeps it running on all cylinders.

were not lovesick forever (see Song of Solomon 2:5). Eventually, reality set in, and their relationship did not last.

I believe the best wisdom to be gleaned from Song of Solomon is the realization that fixating on romance can hoodwink any couple into thinking their marriage is off the mark because they are not constantly starry-eyed and infatuated. Marriage is for grown-ups, not the junior high mentality portrayed in today's average chick flick.

Am I suggesting we strive for marital monotony? No passion and romance, no flowers, no cards, no candlelight dinners? Of course not. There is a place for passion, but passion must be kept in its place. The other side of the marital coin calls for what Peter describes: wives are to respect and appreciate their husbands, and husbands are to esteem, honor, and, yes, respect their wives. I believe God revealed to Peter that marriage is protected, preserved, prized, and pleasurable when two people respect and honor each other. So what should respect look like?

A husband reports that his wife "wrote in my card how much she respects and admires me for what I do for her and our family . . . she tells me this in a lot of different ways on a continuous basis, and each time I'm energized by her words."

A wife tells me, "I seek respect more than love from Jon. He is very affectionate, but I needed Jon to appreciate me for all the things I do for him and accept me for who I am. I am currently the one who has to work so that he can stay in school, who cooks lunch and dinner for him five of the seven days of the week, who makes sure that our finances are in order, who does most of the daily chores—grocery shopping, laundry, cleaning up—who makes sure we don't miss important friends and family dates, and so on."

The hit song asks, "What's love got to do with it?" A great deal, but don't forget respect. If a husband loves his wife as he should, she will feel honored and respected. If a wife respects her husband as she should, he will feel loved and appreciated. It's a win-win. It's love and respect!

PRAYER: Thank the Lord for the truths in 1 Peter 3:1–7, which give the secret to keeping grown-up love alive and well in your marriage. Ask for the wisdom to respect each other as God directs.

ACTION: This week, try to find a copy of the words to Aretha Franklin's hit song from 1965, "R-E-S-P-E-C-T." Try singing it together or at least talk about the words. In various ways tell each other, "I appreciate you," or "I respect what the Lord is doing through you." (For discussion questions, see page 269 in appendix A.)

CHAPTER 51

PLUG INTO THE POWER OF OPTIMISM

PHILIPPIANS 1:6:

Being confident of this, that he who began a good work in you will carry it on to completion until the day of Christ Jesus (NIV).

How optimistic are you about your marriage? We have already seen the importance of being positive about each other (chapter 45), but I am talking about how you see *your marriage*—your commitment as husband and wife to live with love and respect as you glorify Christ.

At Love and Respect Ministries we researched more than twenty-five thousand people and discovered that couples who wish to succeed, and do succeed, have an optimistic outlook on the future of their marriage. Many of these couples have hefty challenges and problems; nonetheless, they feel upbeat. These are some of their comments:

- "We are hopeful that we can have the wonderful marriage we desire, and we are both willing to work on it."

- "We have struggled in our marriage but are hopeful that we can make it work."
- "We have both been reading the book and have never been more excited about our marriage and so hopeful."

By "optimistic," I am not talking about fuzzy-minded naïveté, lack of caution, or poor judgment, nor am I referring to unrealistic and unreasonable enthusiasm. Instead, you have a choice to see the budding prospects of applying love and respect in new and concrete ways. Optimistic couples see the possibility of showing love and respect, even in the face of feeling unloved or disrespected. They refuse to let problems prevent them from applying love and respect, as this husband attests:

> I am *excited* about my wife and our future for the first time in over thirteen years. Truly! A rocky road is still ahead of us, but I now have the knowledge to understand how to feel and how to combat the "no respect" comments from my wife, and hopefully she has the knowledge on the "no love" side as well.

Optimism or pessimism? It is always your choice, no matter what your natural temperament. Some of us are born sanguine (outgoing, cheerful, and positive); others are melancholy (quiet, thoughtful, perhaps brooding). Jeremiah, one of the greatest prophets in the Old Testament, was naturally melancholy, but he still chose optimism in the midst of his anguish over Israel: "This I recall to my mind,/Therefore I have hope./The LORD's lovingkindnesses indeed never cease,/For His compassions never fail./They are new every morning;/Great is Your faithfulness" (Lamentations 3:21–23).

Paul the apostle was far more melancholy than sanguine, yet

in our key verse he says that as Christ followers we can place our confidence in God because He has begun something good, and He will grow and mature His work in us to the end. And remember, Paul wrote Philippians 1:6 while under house arrest, chained to a Roman soldier!

Whether it's Jeremiah or Paul talking, we get some clues about what it means to be optimistic:

- The optimistic have hope in God.
- The optimistic are thankful.
- The optimistic are enthusiastic about what God is doing and will do.

And it is never too late to begin the optimistic journey. One couple, with a less-than-happy marriage for forty-three years, heard the Love & Respect message and were so affected that they became openly affectionate right in front of their adult children. And in an anniversary card the husband told his wife, "I am so excited about our future together!"

That about sums it up. Are you optimistic about your marriage? Then you are excited about your future together, because you know God has started something good and He is only going to make it better!

> INSIGHT: Optimistic couples look forward to a future with love and respect. It works!

PRAYER: Thank the Lord for what He is doing in your marriage and for the hope you have in Him. Ask Him to make you more aware of his unceasing kindnesses and unfailing compassions, which are new every morning. Great is His faithfulness!

ACTION: This week, make it a point to speak optimistically about your marriage. When problems arise, take note of what God is doing, thank Him for what He will do, think positively, and voice these thoughts to one another. (For discussion questions, see page 270 in appendix A.)

CHAPTER 52

WHEN IT'S ALL BEEN SAID AND DONE

PHILIPPIANS 1:21:

For to me, to live is Christ and to die is gain.

To close this book I request your permission to ask an important question. What comes to mind when you read these words?

You are going to die.

Perhaps you are thinking, *Wow, Emerson, what a morbid thought. Nobody is anxious to die.* Well, in one sense that is very true, but in another sense dying should be a glorious thought. If not, what did Paul mean when he said, "For to me, to live is Christ and to die is gain"?

Have you thought about your death or how you will die? Will Shriner said, "I want to die in my sleep like my grand father . . . not screaming and yelling like the passengers in his car." Somewhat dark humor aside, the next time you visit the cemetery, notice the grave markers, each of which includes a birth date and a death date with a dash in between. When you think about it, each person's life comes down to that dash—what went on between birth and death. For Paul, living his dash was about living for Christ. Whatever he did, he did it with Christ in mind.

How does this relate to marriage? As Christ followers, in order for us to live the way Christ calls us to live and do marriage as He intends, we need to catch the vision of coming before Him after death and hearing, "Well done!" (See Matthew 25:14–21.) Envision the scene as believers ascend into heaven and stand before Christ. To one husband He says, "Well done. You put on love when your wife had moments when she was disrespectful, maybe even showing a little contempt. You are about to receive back every act of love you did toward her."

> **INSIGHT:** When it's all been said and done in your marriage, what will God say?

To a wife He says, "Well done. You put on respect toward your husband when he blew it again and was unloving—when you felt dismissed and 'unesteemed.' I watched. You are about to be rewarded for every act of respect."

Almost every week I hear from husbands and wives who have grasped the significance of their "dash." A husband writes:

> My heart was convicted. The reason my marriage was not glorifying God was because I was not living my marriage unto the Lord. It's not about me and my wife having our differences; it's about me living for Christ and dying to myself, submitting my life to God.

Realizing the truth that "my marriage is a trinity" (herself, her husband, and the Lord), one wife writes:

> As I remind myself of loving Christ through my actions and attitudes toward Allen, then everything changes for me. Maybe you could say that I have stepped outside *my* self, *my* reactions, *my* hurt feelings and into the reality of the Lord in our relationship. This truth about Christ being the center of marriage has always been in my thinking. However, through our thirty-two years of marriage, I lived in my own emotional strength. Consequently, the Crazy Cycle rides became more frequent and much longer, but each time I cross over from living only as a "hearer of the Word" to becoming a "doer of the Word," change takes place.

Letters like these tell me that many spouses are getting it when it comes to what they do with their dash. Paraphrasing what Don Moen says in song, when it's all been said and done, only one thing will matter. Did we do our best to live for truth? Did we live for Him, loving and respecting each other unconditionally all the way? Yes, we will have failed now and then. As I pointed out in the first devotional in this book, practicing Love & Respect does not guarantee a marital nirvana. But falling or slipping back is not the issue. *Getting back up is what matters.* Depending on the Lord is the issue. He intends that we let Him work in us every moment, every day. As this book ends, my prayer for you is this:

> Now may the God of peace, who brought from the dead Jesus our Lord, equip you in every way to do His will to love and respect each other as He works in your marriage what is pleasing in His sight, with all glory to Jesus forever and always! Yes! Yes! Yes![1]

PRAYER: Thank the Lord that the Christ follower can say, "For me, to live is Christ and to die is gain." Ask Him for the wisdom and strength to live your "dash" with love and respect for each other.

ACTION: Together or individually, reflect on your marriage over the past several months. What are you building together? How is each of you living out your "dash"? (For discussion questions, see page 272 in appendix A.)

A FINAL WORD ON
REAPING THE REWARDS OF
LOVE & RESPECT

Your Love and Respect Devotional is over—at least for the moment. I hope you will go back and review certain chapters and meditate on the devotional truths you have considered. Some of these devotionals help defeat the Crazy Cycle, and others guide in the use of the powerful principles in the Energizing Cycle. To understand these two cycles is important, even vital:

> Without love she reacts without respect; without respect he reacts without love.

> His love motivates her respect; her respect motivates his love.

Repeatedly, I have opportunity to use the Crazy Cycle analogy to help couples see why they have continuing tension, problems, and fighting. Immediately, they get it. The Energizing Cycle is just as important, but for another reason. While the Crazy Cycle concept is remedial, the Energizing Cycle is proactive. It is a figurative tool kit to help you build your marriage strong and true so that it is able to withstand the onslaughts of the ungodly and demonic forces marshaled against you in these postmodern days of "do what's right in your own eyes."

But please hear me on this next point: while Christ followers can use the concepts in the Crazy Cycle and Energizing Cycle to their fullest potential, even nonbelievers can apply them to stop their fighting and improve their marriage. However, there is much more to the Love & Respect message than that, and this "much more" is found in the Rewarded Cycle. Some of the devotionals in this book are geared directly to helping you get on the Rewarded Cycle, but in truth, I hope all of them will have that long-range effect because the Rewarded Cycle is the heart of the Love & Respect message:

> His love blesses regardless of her respect.
> Her respect blesses regardless of his love.

I hope and pray that as you and your spouse have done the devotionals in this book, you have become aware of its primary purpose: to guide two people to love and respect each other unconditionally, out of a deep consciousness of Jesus Christ. You both realize that marriage is not primarily about pleasing each other, important as that is. Your marriage is about trusting and obeying God's instructions in Ephesians 5:33. You both recognize that your marriage is a tool and a test to deepen and demonstrate your love and reverence for Christ.

As two godly-wise believers you see your marriage as a reflection of the image of God. Together you seek to display the character and strength of Christ before watching family and friends. As a couple you seek to minister as a team and pray as a team. And as you seek the Lord together, you will increasingly see your marriage as God sees your marriage, while He gives you the wisdom and power to do marriage His way.

So I truly hope your Love and Respect Devotional is not over. I hope it is just starting anew as you seek to reap the continuing rewards God has for you.

With Love & Respect,
Emerson

DISCUSSION QUESTIONS
FOR CHAPTERS 1–52

The following questions can be used for individual study, discussion groups, or sparking conversations between husband and wife.

CHAPTER 1: AND THEY LIVED HAPPILY EVER AFTER . . . NOT NECESSARILY

1. Do you agree or disagree that Love & Respect "sounds simple, but it's not so easy to do"? Why is it easy to slip back into old patterns that lead to the Crazy Cycle? How can you help each other be more consistent?

2. The key verse says a righteous spouse "falls seven times, and rises again" (Proverbs 24:16). As you look ahead to practicing Love & Respect, what does this verse mean to you?

   ____ We only get seven chances to mess up.

   ____ God's grace and help are never-ending.

   ____ God is more patient than I deserve.

   ____ I think: _____

3. Which of these three steps seem most helpful when you need to "rise again"?

   ____ Never give up.

   ____ Ask forgiveness of God and each other.

   ____ Ask God for help daily.

   ____ I think: _____

Chapter 2: Pink and Blue: Not Wrong, Just Different!

1. Do you see the Pink and Blue differences between the two of you as a strength or a weakness? How can recognizing these differences be a strength? How can refusing to recognize them cause stress and friction?

2. Do you each agree, deep down, that Pink and Blue are not wrong, just different? Can you thank God for your differences? You may want to jot down the differences that can possibly cause tension and conflict. Discuss them, then make them a matter of definite prayer.

3. Use the Action idea to talk with your spouse about how to help each other see through the other's sunglasses and hear through the other's hearing aids. Is the only time for doing this when you are about to spin on the Crazy Cycle? What are other settings for trying to see each other's viewpoint? What can you do this week to acknowledge and show acceptance of your Pink and Blue differences?

CHAPTER 3: DO YOU HAVE A GOODWILLED MARRIAGE?

1. Why is goodwill such an important principle to understand in your marriage? Can married couples take their goodwill for each other for granted?
2. When is it hardest to seek good and find goodwill in each other? Do certain times of the day come into play? Certain areas of disagreement?
3. Why is it sometimes easy to believe your spouse does not feel goodwill toward you? How often do you find it necessary to give your spouse the "goodwill benefit of the doubt"? How often do you think your spouse has to do the same for you?
4. Why is it vital to always assume your spouse has goodwill toward you, no matter what?

CHAPTER 4: GOD JOINED YOU TOGETHER, AND HE WILL KEEP YOU TOGETHER

1. When you got married, did you believe God brought you together? Think back to how that happened. How was God's hand evident?

2. If God joins us together, why is it still so easy to have conflict, even unhappiness? James 4:1 says that fighting and quarrels come from "desires that battle within you" (NIV). What is the best way to control these desires?

3. In Matthew 19:6, Jesus teaches that man and wife are "no longer two, but one flesh." What does it mean to you to "be one"?

4. How can the Love & Respect Connection keep your marriage bond strong? Do you agree with Emerson and Sarah that "God brought us together and He will keep us together as we do our marriage as unto Him"? Talk together about using the Action item ideas during moments of tension.

CHAPTER 5: THE 80:20 RATIO: THE SECRET TO APPRECIATING YOUR MARRIAGE

1. Emerson says that when he developed the 80:20 ratio, he chose 20 percent as an arbitrary number to estimate the amount of trouble a married couple might have. Do you think that number is too high or too low in relation to your marriage?

2. How do you and your spouse deal with the "many troubles in this life"? (See 1 Corinthians 7:28.)

3. Why is it often easy to focus on the 20 percent (the irritations and annoyances) and forget that most of the time things go quite well? Talk together about the 20 percent times. When do they occur? Why?

4. What do you think of the speech Emerson made to Sarah early in their marriage about how wanting everything to be perfect, but harping on the 20 percent, could poison the 80 percent that was good? Was he too blunt? How did his words affect her?

5. Look at the Action idea for dealing with troubling moments. How would you adapt the suggested wording to apply to your marriage?

CHAPTER 6: MISTAKES HAPPEN—AND THEN WHAT?

1. Is it easy or hard for you to admit you made a mistake? Do you ever try to "wish yourself out of it"?

2. If you make a mistake and offend your spouse, you can choose to do the loving or respectful thing. What would that mean for you personally? What should you do?

3. According to Emerson, there are no more powerful words in marriage than "I was wrong; will you forgive me?" If this is true, why is it sometimes (or often) hard to say them? Which of the following gives you the most trouble?

_____ Anger
_____ Pride
_____ Embarrassment
_____ Fear
_____ Other: _____

4. Ecclesiastes 7:20 says: "There is no one on earth who does what is right all the time and never makes a mistake" (GNT). Is this verse a comfort, a motivator, an encouragement, or a downer? Why?

CHAPTER 7: QUESTION: WHAT IS LOVE? ANSWER: C-O-U-P-L-E

1. How would you answer the question, what is love? Is it something you feel? Something you do? Both? (If you are working together, write down separate answers, then compare.)
2. Emerson teaches husbands that they can love their wives by doing C-O-U-P-L-E: Closeness, Openness, Understanding, Peacemaking, Loyalty, Esteem. Which of these is most important (or perhaps most difficult) for you? (Again, you may want to write separate answers and then compare and discuss.)
3. On a scale of 1 to 10, how well are you riding the Energizing Cycle? Emerson warns not to be discouraged if your score might be better than your spouse's. Choose one of the letters in C-O-U-P-L-E to work on together. For example, how can he be closer? How can she invite his closeness?
4. Note the Action idea at the end of the devotional. Find a tip at the end of chapters 9 through 14 in *Love & Respect* that would be new and different to try.

CHAPTER 8: QUESTION: WHAT IS RESPECT? ANSWER: C-H-A-I-R-S

1. Do you agree with Wendy, who believes "the biggest question or concern women have is, what is respect?" Why do some wives have a hard time respecting their husbands?
2. Should husbands have to earn respect any more than wives have to earn love? Some say unconditional respect (or love) is impossible. Does that mean we shouldn't try?
3. Emerson teaches wives they can respect their husbands by doing C-H-A-I-R-S—appreciating his desire to work and achieve (Conquest), appreciating his desire to protect and provide (Hierarchy), appreciating his desire to lead and serve (Authority), appreciating his desire to analyze and counsel (Insight), appreciating his desire for shoulder-to-shoulder friendship (Relationship), appreciating his desire for physical intimacy (Sexuality). Which of these is most important (or perhaps most difficult) for you? Write separate answers and compare.

CHAPTER 9: NEWTON'S LAW: THE CRAZY CYCLE IN ACTION

1. According to Newton's law, for every action, there is always an equal and opposite reaction. How does this apply to marriage? Give a negative and a positive example.

2. In a locker room incident at military school, Emerson faced Newton's law in a rather painful fashion. Instead of starting a fight, he "threw no punch." Spouses do not exchange physical punches, but it is easy to throw verbal punches or jabs. Proverbs 26:21 warns against being a troublemaker. What does Proverbs 21:23 add concerning tongue control?

3. Why can Newton's Law lead to the Crazy Cycle? Can you state the Crazy Cycle axiom? (Without love she reacts without _____. Without respect, he reacts without _____.) Read the Insight for chapter 9. Why can words be like punches? What kinds of words can get the two of you on the Crazy Cycle?

4. Emerson points out that "your spouse is sensitive and vulnerable." Review the Action item for this devotional. What verbal punches or jabs can you each cut down on?

CHAPTER 10: HE LOVES US BECAUSE HE LOVES US BECAUSE HE LOVES US!

1. Is it easy or hard to truly believe that because you and your spouse are part of God's bride, the church, He will delight in you forever? Describe what it means to you to be part of God's bride, the church.

2. What do Emerson and Sarah do when they are guilty of un-Christlike behavior toward one another? Can you and your spouse join them in saying, "We never give up, because we know He will never give up on us!"

3. Could claiming "God delights in us no matter what" be a cop-out? How do you avoid having that happen? Is appropriating God's forgiveness something you do easily? Do you do it with difficulty? Or with reservations? Read 2 Timothy 2:13 together and talk about it.

4. Review the Action idea. Is there an area where you feel you may have fallen short? Write it down, confess it, then write down a specific way this can help you love or respect your spouse more effectively.

CHAPTER 11: HER PINK PLUS HIS BLUE EQUALS GOD'S PURPLE

1. According to Emerson's word picture, the Blue husband and Pink wife each reflect the image of God, and when they come together they reflect Purple—God's color of royalty. What does this imagery do for your view of your marriage?

2. Does Pink and Blue blending into God's Purple help explain the mystery of two becoming "one flesh" (Ephesians 5:31)? Many people say this verse refers to coming together sexually. Why must it mean more than that?

3. Emerson writes: "In marriage he and she become a 'we.' The husband doesn't lose his masculinity, nor does the wife lose her femininity. But together they are more—much more!" How do husband and wife become "more" in their marriage? Which of the following statements apply to you and your spouse?

   _____ We become more of a team.
   _____ We can know greater depths of love and respect.
   _____ We can honor Christ more.
   _____ We can feel oneness even when things aren't perfect.
   _____ I think: _____

4. How can your oneness (Purpleness) be diluted?

   _____ We slip back on to the Crazy Cycle.
   _____ We don't do enough of the Energizing Cycle.
   _____ I forget Christ is listening.
   _____ I neglect my personal prayer life.

5. Talk together about the Action item. In what other ways can you keep your Pink and Blue a strong shade of Purple?

CHAPTER 12: IT'S ALL ABOUT PERSPECTIVE

1. Do you remember the 80:20 ratio from chapter 5? We can expect troubles at least 20 percent of the time in our marriage (sometimes more, sometimes less), but around 80 percent of the time the experiences in our marriage will be good. Why is perspective so important in not letting the 20 percent put us on the Crazy Cycle?

2. According to Emerson, concentrating on the 80 percent will keep the Energizing Cycle going strong. What does the Energizing Cycle axiom say? (His love motivates her _____. Her respect motivates his _____.) How many specific things have you done in the past month to put emphasis on the positive 80 percent and motivate his love and her respect? (You may want to review the C-O-U-P-L-E and C-H-A-I-R-S acronyms: see chapters 7 and 8.)

3. How can memorizing Proverbs 12:16 keep the Energizing Cycle humming? How hard is "shrugging off insults" (or overlooking minor offenses) for you?

4. Reread the story of the farmer's muddy boots in chapter 12. Then discuss the statement, "Perspective *is* everything!"

CHAPTER 13: THOSE WHO PRAY TOGETHER LEARN TO LOVE & RESPECT TOGETHER

1. We all know prayer is important to a marriage, but 55 percent of Love & Respect couples report that they do not pray together. Reasons spouses often list for not praying together include these:

   - Don't want to be "prayed at"
   - Seems awkward
   - Tried it and then gave it up

   If any of these apply to you, talk about it and share your hearts.

2. Forty-five percent of Love & Respect couples *do* report praying together and reaping benefits such as better communication and enjoying more dates and sex together. Is "reaping benefits" the best motivation for praying? Why should you and your spouse try to pray together on a regular basis? (Note why Emerson and Sarah pray together.)

3. Jesus taught His disciples always to pray and not to get discouraged ("lose heart"). What causes you to lose heart in praying? Why? What will you do to encourage yourself to keep praying?

4. According to Emerson, God sends three basic answers to prayer: "yes," "no," and "wait awhile." How do you deal with "no" or "wait awhile"? Is it sometimes hard to tell the difference? Could what seems to be "no" really be God saying, "Wait and trust Me"?

5. If you have not been praying together, note the suggestions

in the Action item for this devotional. Are you willing to try praying together, being careful to make each other as comfortable as possible?

CHAPTER 14: WHO IS ON YOUR MENTAL COMMITTEE?

1. Everyone has a "mental committee" called "they" whose opinions matter. Name some of the "they" people in your life from whom you hope to get approval.

2. When trying to practice Love & Respect, why is it possible to run into open or subtle opposition from friends and family, most of whom are probably on your mental committee?

3. Saul, a Pharisee of Pharisees, believed in Christ and became Paul the apostle, causing his former friends and colleagues to criticize him severely and worse. What kept Paul from being concerned when "they" came after him? (Review Galatians 1:10.)

4. Talk with your spouse about how your decision to practice Love & Respect has been received by family and friends. If you have no opposition, and only encouragement, thank God. If there are critics whose opinions matter, discuss how to remove them from your mental committee as lovingly and peacefully as possible.

CHAPTER 15: TO TELL THE TRUTH . . . IS NOT ALWAYS EASY

1. Can practicing Love & Respect lead to trying to be "too nice"—to not being honest about what is bothering you? Have either of you been doing this to avoid conflict and keep the peace? Share your thoughts—with love and respect.
2. Is there also a danger in being "too honest"? Talk about how you can be honest—but gentle—with each other.
3. In the Old Testament and the New, God puts a premium on telling the truth. What does that tell you about your relationship with Him and with each other? (See Ephesians 4:25 and the endnote in chapter 15 about Zechariah 8:16.)
4. What do you think of the idea in the Action item to leave little signs around the house saying, "Talk to me like you *love* me," and "Talk to me like you *respect* me"? Think of other ways you can remember this principle: if I love (or respect) my spouse, I will speak truthfully, and my truthful speech will be loving or respectful.

CHAPTER 16: FEELINGS AREN'T FACTS—ALWAYS SORT IT OUT

1. Why is it important to balance feelings against the facts? What makes it hard to do this? How can you help each other with this issue?
2. How can remembering that you are a combination of Pink and Blue, and that nobody is wrong, just different, help you balance the "fact versus feelings" scale?
3. Sometimes your feelings can become so strong that you "just know" you are right and your spouse is wrong. Reread what the devotional says about Proverbs 16:25 and how venting strong feelings is the "road to ruin" of the moment, the day, the evening, and so on. Talk together about how to process what "seems right" with love and respect.
4. The Action item suggests that when someone's feelings are strong, that person should describe his or her feelings while the other one listens carefully. To get started, one of you could say, "We are about to spin on the Crazy Cycle. Let's talk about my feelings and try to get to the facts." What is the best way to say this? What should you guard against?

Chapter 17: What Is Really Going on Here?

1. When things get a little tense between you, do you ever sense that the *apparent* issue (what to buy, where to go, where to turn, and so on) isn't the real issue? How can realizing that someone doesn't feel loved or respected help you deal with the issue at hand and make a decision you both can live with?

2. Read together the scene between Jacob and Rachel in Genesis 30:1–2. What did Jacob miss in her desperate cry? Why was she so desperate? (It will help to read Genesis 29 and the rest of 30 to get the entire dysfunctional picture.) What was the bottom line in this scene in Love & Respect terms?

3. How can memorizing Proverbs 15:13 help you be more alert to situations when what seems to be the issue isn't the real issue?

4. Discuss the Action item. Would this be difficult or easy to do? Why? Is it worth trying?

CHAPTER 18: JOHN WOODEN: A LOVE & RESPECT LEGACY FOR THE AGES

1. John Wooden's athletic achievements were legendary, but what made him such an outstanding human being was that he lived by biblical principles. What can you take from John Wooden's legacy that you can use to live your marriage with love and respect?

2. How does the following quote by John Wooden apply to you as a spouse? "You can't live a perfect day without doing something for someone who will never be able to repay you."[1] What habits or practices described in C-O-U-P-L-E or C-H-A-I-R-S (see chapters 7 and 8) can you improve or develop to become more unconditionally loving or respectful?

3. John Wooden also said, "Consider the rights of others before your own feelings, and the feelings of others before your own rights." How does this quote parallel the following questions from *Love & Respect*?

   "Is what I am about to say or do going to feel unloving to her?"

   "Is what I am about to say or do going to feel disrespectful to him?"

4. Proverbs 3:35 promises: "The wise will have glory for their heritage" (BBE). Have you thought much about the heritage or legacy you want to pass on to those who come after you? Take time to use the Action item and write down the legacy you want to leave behind. Then compare what you both have written and use the Prayer suggestions to trust yourself anew to Jesus.

CHAPTER 19: FORGET THE NEGATIVE SNAPSHOTS— ENJOY THE POSITIVE MOVIE

1. Does the "snapshot versus movie" analogy fit your marriage? Why is it easy to let the negative snapshots overshadow the positive ongoing movie? What emotions are often involved?

2. Emerson says concentrating on the "local snapshot" can lead to a very negative "global judgment." How do Jesus' words in Matthew 7:1-3 apply?

3. When someone writes to Emerson and lists a number of negative snapshots of his or her spouse, Emerson suggests listing five to ten positive things instead. Why does this simple exercise frequently change the judgmental person's perception?

4. Sometimes the negative snapshots just seem to keep happening. Use the Action item to talk together about why you are feeling unloved or disrespected. Remember, you are goodwilled people, starring in a long-running movie!

CHAPTER 20: SEX AND AFFECTION: A TWO-WAY STREET

1. What, in your opinion, is the best way to see sex? As a "duty" or as something to be fair about? How can you be fairer or more reasonable about having sex? What does Emerson mean when he says, "Fair play should always precede foreplay"?

2. How do you respond to Emerson's request to look at the sexual aspect of your relationship as a compliment to how important you are in your spouse's life? You are the only one who can meet this need in your spouse! Have you ever thought about it this way before?

3. Read 1 Corinthians 7:3–5, noting especially the concept of the wife's body not belonging to herself alone and the husband's body not belonging to himself alone. How does this passage throw light on what it means to be "one flesh" (see Ephesians 5:31; Matthew 19:6)?

4. As the Action item points out, sex can be a sensitive subject. Is sex a big enough issue in your marriage that you should consider seeing a godly-wise counselor who has helped other couples adjust sexually? (See appendix D on page 289 for counseling resources.)

Chapter 21: Keep Your Eyes on the Lord, Not the Problem

1. Are you and your spouse facing any "what do we do now?" problems at the moment? If so, have you talked about them together? On a scale of 1 to 10, to what degree are you facing these problems "with your eyes on the Lord"?

2. Why can problems cause friction and tension between Pink and Blue? What can you do to blend into Purple? Why can this make you stronger as a couple?

3. In 2 Chronicles, chapter 20, you can see how the Israelites faced an overwhelming force and not only survived but won. But Scripture records that they didn't always win. How are we to respond if we try to keep our eyes on God, but the problem is too big or too powerful?

4. Use the Action item to assess any problems you may be facing. How are these problems affecting your attempts to treat each other with unconditional love and respect? If you have no problems right now, prepare for what may come by reminding each other: "The battle is not ours, but the Lord's!"

CHAPTER 22: OUR "GOOD" MAY BE WILLING, BUT OUR FLESH CAN BE WEAK

1. Read again the examples given by Emerson and Sarah about starting out the day intending to love and respect each other and then having things go wrong. Do similar things happen to you? Share with each other how this makes you feel and why it is important to keep reminding yourself, *my spouse really does have goodwill toward me.*

2. When your spouse fails to carry out good intentions, how much does it help to hear: "You know I have goodwill, don't you? Please forgive me. I blew it again." Is it easy to forgive? What would you rather hear your spouse say?

3. What was Paul's answer to his "flesh is weak" dilemma in Romans 7:15–20? (See Romans 8:1–6.) What must the Christ follower never forget if he or she wants to let the Spirit have control? (See especially verses 1–2.)

4. The road to the Crazy Cycle can be paved with good intentions. Use the Action item to discuss the best ways to help each other fulfill good intentions and show goodwill. What obvious practice can you both engage in to remind yourselves, *I have goodwill and so does my spouse?*

CHAPTER 23: EXCUSE ME, IS THAT YOUR FOOT ON MY AIR HOSE?

1. On page 306 of *Love & Respect*, Emerson suggests the following "canned" ways to let your spouse know you have been offended or hurt:

   "That felt unloving. Did I just come across as disrespectful?"
   "That felt disrespectful. Did I just come across as unloving?"

   Some spouses report that these statements feel awkward. Why do you think this could be so? Would it be less confrontational to say, "Excuse me, is that your foot on my air hose?" Why or why not?

2. Remember, the air hose word picture works in two situations: if you are trying to let your spouse know you are offended, or if you want to find out if *you* may have done the offending. In Ecclesiastes 10:12, Solomon observed, "It is pleasant to listen to wise words, but the speech of fools brings them to ruin." None of us want to use the speech of a fool. How can the air hose word picture qualify as a wise way to communicate when you see your spouse's spirit deflate? ("Hey, I am detecting I may have stepped on your air hose. If so, I am really sorry. Tell me what you are thinking.")

3. Have you ever used the air hose metaphor to defuse tension? Why or why not? Is there a better way to break the ice and let your spouse know you may have been offended or hurt? If you haven't been using it, are you willing to try?

4. Use the Action item and discuss why saying "That's your problem" is foolish speech, while admitting "This is our

problem" is a wise way to stay off each other's air hose. Which of the following is the best way to suggest, "This is our problem"?

_____ "This is our problem because we are a goodwilled team that always works together."

_____ "This is our problem. I want to know what I might be doing to help cause it."

_____ "This is our problem. Let's solve it together."

CHAPTER 24: IT'S HARD TO BE NEGATIVE WHILE BEING THANKFUL

1. On a scale of 1 to 10 (10 meaning "extremely"), how thankful are you for each other? How often do you express it to each other? What kind of a limit does 1 Thessalonians 5:18 put on being thankful?
2. When Sarah's son, David, badly damaged his leg, she got strength and help by offering "a sacrifice of thanksgiving" (Psalm 50:23). Does this sound like something you would want to try? When could this be a difficult thing to do?
3. Do you agree that it is hard to be negative while being thankful in all circumstances? What if circumstances don't change?
4. If thanksgiving has not been a big part of your prayer time, use the Action item and start the practice of offering a sacrifice of thanksgiving and praise, not necessarily *for* the circumstances but *in* the circumstances. Christ Jesus knows all about your circumstances and He cares for you!

CHAPTER 25: DON'T BELIEVE EVERYTHING YOUR SPOUSE SAYS (ESPECIALLY IN ANGER)

1. Do you ever say things to each other you don't necessarily mean? When does this usually occur and why?
2. How much does body language (facial expression, tone of voice) have to do with saying something you don't really mean?
3. Looking at the decoding issue from the other side, is it really fair to your spouse to always say, "Don't be so gullible—you know I didn't mean it"? Should one spouse have to constantly decode the other? Where is the balance in responsibility? How can love and respect play a role in helping you both find this balance?
4. Use the Action item to talk together about what it means to decode and what it means to send messages the other can trust.

Chapter 26: Forgiveness, Part I: Love & Respect Takes Two Good Forgivers

1. Why does Ruth Graham's statement that a good marriage takes two good forgivers apply especially when it comes to stopping the Crazy Cycle? Where is forgiveness when the two of you are on the CC or just about to go there?

2. We know Scripture teaches us to forgive and make allowances for each other's faults (Colossians 3:13), but we can give good reasons (to ourselves) why we can't forgive (at least not right away). Which of these sounds like you?

   _____ "I don't deserve to be treated this way! This is unfair!"
   _____ "I can't let my spouse off the hook for this. Justice must be served!"
   _____ "I have a right to feel this way. Jesus understands what I go through."
   _____ Other: _____

   Why don't any of the above cut it with Jesus? (See Matthew 6:15.)

3. How often must you forgive each other? Isn't there some kind of standard? (See Matthew 18:21.)

4. Many of us battle a tendency to be too quick to take offense. Use the Action item and talk together about practicing "quick forgiveness" instead.

CHAPTER 27: FORGIVENESS, PART II: GOT FORGIVENESS? LET JESUS BE YOUR MODEL

1. As you consider following in Jesus' steps to be more forgiving, which of the following is hardest for you and why?

    • To sympathize with my spouse (to try to understand the behavior)
    • To relinquish the offense to God (to let it go)

    Talk together about these ways to follow Jesus. The more you talk, the easier it will be to forgive!

2. How can remembering the principle of goodwill help you to forgive?

3. Why is it important to let Jesus be your model? Also, does forgiving always lead to kissing and making up?

4. Forgiveness can be a delicate subject. Go through the Action item and use ideas that may apply to your situation at the moment.

CHAPTER 28: NO MATTER HOW YOU FEEL, TRUST SCRIPTURE MORE THAN YOUR FEELINGS

1. Why are feelings more important to many people than what is written down in the authoritative source, the Bible?
2. How valid is the argument that you should follow your feelings because your feelings are real? Are Christians robots who must deny their feelings in order to obey God?
3. Children have real feelings too. What does 1 Corinthians 33:11 say about dealing with "childish ways"?
4. How important is Scripture in becoming mature in Christ? What do the following Scriptures mean to you?

- 2 Timothy 3:16: "All Scripture is inspired by God and profitable for teaching, for reproof, for correction, for training in righteousness."
- 1 Thessalonians 2:13: "For this reason we also constantly thank God that when you received the word of God which you heard from us, you accepted it not as the word of men, but for what it really is, the word of God, which also performs its work in you who believe."
- Matthew 4:4: "But He answered and said, 'It is written, "MAN SHALL NOT LIVE ON BREAD ALONE, BUT ON EVERY WORD THAT PROCEEDS OUT OF THE MOUTH OF GOD."'"

Talk about how difficult it would be to practice Love & Respect without viewing Scripture as God's absolutely authoritative Word of Truth.

CHAPTER 29: REMEMBER, GOD DESIGNED YOUR SPOUSE—BE PATIENT!

1. Have you ever thought about how God has designed you for each other? What attracted you to each other? Can you see how you complement each other in different ways?

2. No marriage or spouse is perfect. Can you talk together quietly about what you do that annoys or irritates the other? What should the annoyer do? What should the one who gets annoyed do? Where and how does love and respect enter in?

3. The apostle Paul says patience includes humility, gentleness, tolerance, and love (Ephesians 4:1). Which is most important? Or does it depend on the situation?

4. Use the Action item to talk about what it means to be patient with each other in different situations and at different times of the day. If you have children, talk about how they can wear on one's patience and how you can give each other support in your different parenting roles.

Chapter 30: Impact Others with Love & Respect

1. If you have not taken time to discuss the opening question in the devotional, do so now. How has Love & Respect impacted your marriage? Could you be ready to start sharing what you have learned with other couples?

2. Emerson points out that he knows of many couples who get more out of Love & Respect by facilitating a group than they did practicing L&R alone. Why do you think this might be true for some couples? Could it be true for you?

3. In 1 Corinthians 12:6 the apostle Paul is speaking of how God works in His body in many different ways. The Love & Respect Connection has made an impact on many churches and helped couples develop lasting relationships as they have worked on their marriages together. Could this be something that God wants to do in your church?

4. To use the Action item, visit http://loveandrespect.com/store to order resources. Talk about which items would be most beneficial in assessing how you might get an L&R group started.

CHAPTER 31: MUTUAL SUBMISSION, SEX, AND TUESDAY NIGHT

1. Discuss Emerson's second paragraph, in which he defines mutual submission. According to Emerson, "Mutual submission is less about specific decisions and more about attitude. . . . By practicing love and respect, mutual submission is possible." Do you agree or disagree? Share your ideas.

2. Do you agree or disagree that mutual authority regarding sex can lead to mutual submission? In what sense?

3. Many couples have told Emerson that they literally develop a schedule for having sex a certain number of days a week, in addition to scheduling time for prayer and talking together. The idea is that what works for the goose can work for the gander. What are the advantages and disadvantages of this kind of plan? Could it take the guesswork out of your sexual and emotional relationship as you mutually submit to each other's needs?

CHAPTER 32: ANGER CAN BE DANGEROUS . . . HANDLE WITH CARE

1. Emerson writes in the second paragraph: "I believe there is no more dangerous emotion for a married couple to deal with than anger." Do you both agree? What other emotions are hard for you to deal with?

2. When marital tension cranks up and frustration is turning to anger, why is slipping into "default mode" a real possibility? How much does rationalization have to do with allowing yourself to slip into default mode? What does James 1:20 have to say about rationalizing angry language and behavior?

3. What do you think of Emerson's idea to repeat Proverbs 14:29 three times as a way to control angry feelings? Could this work for you? Are you willing to try it?

Chapter 33: All Things Do Work Together for Good . . . Sooner or Later

1. What do you make of the story of the swallowed contact lens? Was it just a coincidence that Emerson only needed one new contact, that the old one that was left was just right for one of his eyes? What if he had needed two new contacts? Would Romans 8:28 not have been true in that situation?

2. Sarah and Emerson rejoiced in the news that he needed only one new contact and saw it as an example of how God makes all things work together for good for those who love Him, even the mundane stuff. When you are trusting God, what is the difference between mundane stuff and important stuff?

3. Emerson concludes by saying, "He does work things out for good—sooner or later." Do you agree? How much later can God work it out? Would it be fair to say that God can works things out now here on earth or later in Heaven? What about the believers described in Hebrews 11:13?

4. Use the Action item and talk about the best way to respond when bad things happen. How much of a role does prayer play in your marriage? Should it have a more important place? (Review chapter 13, "Those Who Pray Together Learn to Love & Respect Together.")

CHAPTER 34: DO YOU SEEK TO UNDERSTAND OR ONLY WANT TO BE UNDERSTOOD?

1. A major hurdle to reaching mutual understanding and better communication is being Pink and Blue. One husband put it plainly: "I am Blue and you are Pink, so get over it. I am not supposed to understand you." A lot of husbands might agree. How did his wife answer him? Was she respectful?

2. Emerson asserts that it is more important to understand your spouse than be understood. What does this have to do with love and respect?

3. When seeking to understand your spouse, why is James 1:19 good advice? Which quality mentioned in the verse is most important for you? Being quick to listen? Being slow to speak? Being slow to become angry? For additional wise advice, compare Proverbs 18:13: "He who answers before listening—that is his folly and his shame" (NIV).

4. Discuss the "seeking to understand" idea in the Action item. The lead-in line, "What I hear you saying is . . . Am I correct?" is a familiar one that is often suggested in communication seminars. Can it work for you and your spouse? Would it help to put it in the context of love and respect?

CHAPTER 35: IT *IS* ALL ABOUT ME, AFTER ALL

1. Do you ever think about what it means to live in a postmodern culture? Postmodernists claim that there is no absolute truth, that anyone's "truth" is as good and as true as anyone else's. How can this attitude eat away at your marriage? How can you prevent that from happening?

2. One researcher tried to assess what a "happy" marriage is by asking:

   - How much does your partner provide a source of exciting experiences?
   - How much has knowing your partner made you a better person?

   Why are these questions a trap for the Christian couple?

3. Is it always wrong or dangerous to ask, what's in it for me? What question must come first?

4. Use the Action item and talk about how effective it might be to remember the words on your reminder notes: "It *is* all about me." In what sense is this always true?

CHAPTER 36: WHO MAKES THE FIRST MOVE IN YOUR MARRIAGE?

1. What is the great strength in believing that the more mature spouse will move first to end a stalemate? What is a possible weakness and source of friction?

2. According to Emerson, "Mature moves by goodwilled spouses positively influence the marriage in God's direction." Do you believe this statement is true or false? (This may sound like a no-brainer, but why is it a no-brainer? How does Hebrews 5:14 help explain it?)

3. The mature one should move first, but what does that look like? Emerson gives several examples. Can you think of what you might typically do to make the first move?

4. Do you believe that the two of you can (or should) take turns making the first move? Use the Action item to talk about how it feels when one of you makes the first move. Is this a time to express gratitude with love and respect?

CHAPTER 37: TO OVERCOME THE PAST, FOCUS ON THE PRIZE

1. An NFL coach says that his way of dealing with adversity is to "keep your eye on the prize." Is this an equally good strategy for you in your marriage? Do you see yourself and your spouse as a team that has wins and losses? In what sense? With what or whom are you competing?

2. In Philippians 3:13–14, Paul compares the Christian life to a race or contest. Does he say that we have to finish first to receive the prize? What *is* he saying? How does this apply to your marriage?

3. Emerson says that because of your faith in Christ, you and your spouse are loved, win or lose, and no matter what happens you must never see yourselves as losers when you fail to love or respect and the Crazy Cycle starts up. What is Paul's instruction about dealing with the past in Philippians 3:13?

4. What is the most encouraging phrase or statement in this devotional for you and your marriage?

   _____ Marriage is a marathon, not a dash.
   _____ Always keep your eye on the prize.
   _____ In Christ, you are loved—win, lose, or tie.
   _____ Never see yourself as a loser.

5. The Action item suggests that you agree together to deal with setbacks by saying, "Forget yesterday's loss. Let's focus on today's opportunity, because of tomorrow's prize." How can you make this a continuing motto—perhaps a code of sorts—that you both can use to encourage each other?

CHAPTER 38: IS MY RESPONSE *ALWAYS* MY RESPONSIBILITY?

1. According to Emerson, when your spouse provokes you by doing something unloving or disrespectful, and you respond in kind, it does not *cause* you to be the way you are, it *reveals* the way you are. Do you agree or disagree?
2. Is Emerson saying that you must be perfect and never get provoked? What should you do when you feel like the wife who sometimes just wants "to disappear him"?
3. No matter what your spouse says or does, you have a choice to respond with love or respect, or to respond without it. As a Christ follower, do you have to make that choice alone? (See John 8:31–32, 36.)
4. Discuss the Action item. Would putting up reminders saying "My response is my responsibility" be something that would definitely help you? Why not try it for a week or so and then compare notes? Should this reminder be made into a permanent sign or plaque and displayed in a prominent place in your home?

CHAPTER 39: LOOK! JUST OVER YOUR SPOUSE'S SHOULDER! IT'S JESUS!

1. Have you thought much about the principle, "Whatever I do for my spouse, I do for Christ as well"? (See Matthew 25:40.) Is this encouraging, or perhaps a bit intimidating? Share your thoughts and concerns with your spouse.

2. What does envisioning Christ just over your spouse's shoulder, listening to every conversation you have, do for you? What kind of look might be on Jesus' face as He hears you talking?

   ____ Stern disapproval
   ____ Mild displeasure
   ____ Bemused wonder
   ____ Smiling approval

   You might point out, "It would depend on what I was saying, how I was acting." (Bingo! You get it.) Talk together about the power of this word picture.

3. But suppose word pictures are not your thing and you tend to forget that Christ is listening just beyond your spouse's shoulder. Which of the following reminder ideas might work, stuck to your mirror or computer screen?

   ____ "Do I love (or respect) my spouse as unto Him?"
   ____ "Look! Just over (spouse's name) shoulder! It's Jesus!"
   ____ "When I do it for my spouse, I do it for Him."

   Your goal is not trying to make Jesus smile at gimmicks. You want to remember something important. Talk together about the truth of this devotional. What is the Lord trying to tell each of you? Both of you?

4. Emerson closes this devotional with a reference to the power of the Rewarded Cycle. Why is the Rewarded Cycle the heart and soul of the Love & Respect Connection? Can you repeat the RC axiom?

His love blesses regardless of her _____.
Her respect blesses regardless of his _____.

5. How important to the Rewarded Cycle is loving and respecting *unconditionally*? Should *anything* be able to cause us to be unloving or disrespectful? Can any person ever force us to show an attitude of hostility and contempt, or is that always our choice?

CHAPTER 40: IF ONLY WE DIDN'T HAVE MONEY PROBLEMS

1. Many marriage experts cite money mismanagement as a main source of marital discord, but Emerson says the root reason lies elsewhere. Money is a serious issue, but what is always the Real Issue that shortage of money brings out?

2. Do you agree that fighting over money only reveals what is in our hearts, how immature we really are? Have you ever thought about it that way?

3. Philippians 4:19 promises God will supply all our needs. What is the difference between needs and wants? Is figuring this out a crucial part of managing money? Why do couples have trouble with this? Who is in charge of money in your marriage? Do you work together on your budget at some point?

4. Use the Action item and work together to sort out your needs from your wants. See this as a wonderful opportunity to work as a team, to grow together as a Love & Respect couple. If you have serious complications because of overspending, emergency expenses, or a job loss, you may need the help of a financial counselor. (See appendix D on page 289 for counseling resources.)

CHAPTER 41: YOUR SPOUSE HAS NEEDS ONLY YOU CAN FILL

1. On a scale of 1 to 10, how much do you put your spouse's needs ahead of your own? What are your measuring sticks? Compare notes with each other. How is each of you doing in this area?

2. What is involved in putting your spouse's needs ahead of your own? As you read the examples of what Sarah does for Emerson and vice versa, who appears to be making the bigger sacrifice? Can something like this ever be measured accurately? What part does personal time play? Which is more important? Provide physical assistance or spend your time? Or do they usually go together?

3. What does Paul say should be your real motivation for trying to meet each other's needs ahead of your own? (See the key verse.) Talk together about imitating Jesus as you seek to meet each other's needs, and about allowing Him to renew and grow your thoughts and attitudes. (See Ephesians 4:23.)

4. Talk about the Action item idea of saying "Thanks for the compliment" in response to each other's requests and needs. Why is being asked to take out the trash or iron a shirt a compliment?

CHAPTER 42: BUT IS YOUR SPOUSE SUPPOSED TO MEET *ALL* YOUR NEEDS?

1. Your spouse cannot possibly meet *all* your needs. Is this disappointing? A relief? When you got married, did you think, *now all my needs will be met*? What *did* you think?

2. How does the 80:20 ratio help explain why a spouse cannot meet all the needs of his or her partner?

3. Emerson observes that it "takes maturity to realize that difficulties and disappointments are not exceptions; they are quite often the rule. . . . Moments like these can be wake-up calls asking both of you to realize that your deepest contentment and peace are in Christ, not in each other." Do you agree? Talk about it and also consider the good news in Hebrews 4:16 and 2 Corinthians 12:9–10.

4. Use the Action item to talk about the difference between needing each other and ultimately depending on the Lord. How can practicing Love & Respect help you sort it out?

CHAPTER 43: YOUR CHILDREN ARE WATCHING

1. No sincere Christ follower would agree with little Billy, who supposedly defined faith as "believing something that you know isn't true." A "counterdefinition" might be that faith is believing something you hope *is* true. How would you define faith? What scripture passages come to mind?

2. Do you agree that you and your spouse play the most vital role in passing along the faith to your children? Why? What about pastors and Sunday school teachers? What do Mom and Dad have that they don't have?

3. What are some good ways to live out Deuteronomy 11:18–19 with your children? Choose those listed here that apply, and write in your own ideas.

    _____ Pray openly before them at different times about family concerns.

    _____ Use teachable moments to talk about spiritual truths you are learning.

    _____ Be openly loving and affectionate toward each other.

    _____ Always be openly loving and affectionate with your children, assuring them of your love and God's.

    _____ Other: _____

4. Choose any of the following questions from chapter 43 and talk together about your responsibility to communicate your faith to your children.

    _____ Do our children see us face problems with peace and contentment or worry and anger?

_____ In our marriage, is there real love and respect? Do our children see it?

_____ Do our kids see us as "the real deal" when it comes to following Jesus?

CHAPTER 44: I AM *NOT* BEING DEFENSIVE!

1. Why is it sometimes easy to offend each other without even trying? Correcting each other, asking each other to make a change of some kind—these are typical causes of defensiveness. So is it best not to say anything at all? What *is* best?
2. How much of a problem is "getting defensive" for you? For your spouse? What does feeling unloved or disrespected have to do with getting defensive?
3. Proverbs 18:19 warns that it is harder to made amends with an offended friend (possibly your spouse) than to capture a fortified city. What does this commentary on human nature tell you about the importance of always trying to be loving and respectful? About being humble and forgiving?
4. Use the Action idea to talk together about the fine line between being defensive and then taking the offensive and going on the Crazy Cycle. If offended, what is your best move?

CHAPTER 45: HOW POSITIVE ARE YOU WITH EACH OTHER?

1. As the devotional asks, on a scale of 1 to 10, how positive are you with your spouse? Does the number go up when you look at your spouse through God's eyes?
2. Read Philippians 4:8 slowly. What is the key to thinking all these positive thoughts? (See Philippians 4:6–7.) Can you depend only on yourself to control your thoughts?
3. Do you agree that focusing on the positive takes discipline? Why is it easier for some people than others? If you naturally tend to see the glass half empty, what can you do?
4. Use the Action idea to talk about what you see in each other that is excellent and praiseworthy. Does Philippians 4:8 say we must overlook negative things that need to be dealt with? What is the best way to deal with negatives? This might be a good time to review chapter 19, "Forget the Negative Snapshots—Enjoy the Positive Movie."

CHAPTER 46: DO YOU EVER PLAY THE BLAME GAME?

1. The blame game is as old as Adam and Eve. Why is it hard to take the blame, especially when you "just know" it was not your fault?

2. We know our response is our responsibility, but we still want to pass the buck. Is it possible that we hold some reservations about taking *all* the blame? After all, aren't there always two sides to everything?

3. God has been getting the blame for a lot of things since He put Adam and Eve in the garden. In fact, how did Adam blame God for his sin? (See Genesis 3:12.) Emerson admits, "How like Adam I can be at times." Do you identify? In what kinds of situations are you tempted to come up with the same kind of lame excuse that Adam gave?

4. Pro golfer Barb Whitehead admits that when she made a bad shot or missed a putt, she had no one to blame but herself. She compares golf to her marriage, saying, "In the end I have to answer to the Lord about what I did with the man God gave me." Barb adds that this is not pressure; instead, it is freeing because she always has a choice. Talk together about Barb's approach to her marriage, and why practicing Love & Respect can help end the blame game.

CHAPTER 47: GROUPTHINK CAN BE TOXIC TO YOUR MARRIAGE

1. Do you ever run into groupthink at work, on the golf course or tennis court, or even at Uncle Harry's house? What are the characteristics of groupthink? Why is it the antithesis of love and respect?
2. How does the principle that Pink and Blue are not wrong, just different, counter groupthink stereotypes? Since God clearly made us male and female, isn't it rather foolish to make fun of His handiwork?
3. According to this devotional, what is the difference between groupthink and Godthink? Try writing separate definitions, then compare ideas.

CHAPTER 48: DO YOU KNOW HOW TO FIGHT FAIR?

In lieu of the usual discussion questions, here are rules for
fighting fair. Which of the following suggestions can you and
your spouse use to disagree more agreeably? Accompanying
each "rule" is a quote by a husband or wife testifying what to
do or not do to avoid the world's unfair dog-eat-dog way of
fighting. (See 2 Corinthians 10:3 MSG.)

_____ Remember that this argument (or fight) is only that—
one disagreement. ("I have to remember that one disagreement is not the end of the world. We're getting it,
slowly but surely.")

_____ Stay on the current topic—don't get "historical." ("I don't
just talk about recent angry feelings, but go all the way
back to the beginning. He may do something that is
unloving, and I immediately think back to all the other
instances, and it confirms that 'he doesn't really love
me.' I set my husband up for failure.")

_____ Keep it private—do not let any "fighting fallout" land on
the kids. ("We have harmed our children from all the
years of fighting.")

_____ Remind each other that you are allies, not enemies;
goodwilled, not ill-willed. ("I have stopped aiming my
weapons at him and taken aim at the true enemy trying to destroy our marriage. We fight on the same team
now.")

_____ Argue with win-win in mind. ("We voice feelings and
ideas in a way that leads to some kind of solution that
works for both of us. We find that when we set our

negative emotions aside for a moment, we come up with a third option we both like.")

_____ Apologize when you are wrong. ("When my spouse admits wrongdoing, I let her step away from the argument without humiliation. I let her save face.")

CHAPTER 49: YOUR WORDS REVEAL YOUR HEART

1. Reread the examples of how Emerson and Sarah might get distracted when trying to communicate. If it is true that words reveal the heart, is it not equally true that what we don't say due to selfish distractions also reveals the heart? Is getting distracted a permanent condition or really a bad habit that can be broken?

2. James 3:2 is a familiar verse. Which of the following is a good way to "control the tongue"? Choose more than one, and add your own ideas.

   _____ Pay attention and listen carefully.

   _____ Bite your tongue (be slow to speak).

   _____ Seek to speak less imperfectly.

   _____ Stop to pray, then speak.

   _____ Other: _____

3. Emerson does not believe that seeking to speak less imperfectly is aiming too low. Do you agree? Why or why not?

4. Try the Action idea for a number of days, then talk together about how hard (or surprisingly easy) it has been to focus your attention and measure your words.

CHAPTER 50: WHY WE ALL NEED RESPECT

1. Emerson claims that love may make the world go round, but love is not sufficient to make a marriage work. According to research gathered at Love & Respect conferences, what else is needed—by Pink as well as Blue? One wife made this remark: "I feel I receive a lot of love from him, but I also need respect and appreciation." Is this feeling typical among wives?

2. In 1 Peter 3:1–7, Peter's powerful passage on the intimacy of marriage, the apostle says nothing about "love" but a lot about respect. Emerson concludes: "I believe God revealed to Peter that marriage is protected, preserved, prized, and pleasurable when two people respect and honor each other." Is he saying that a marriage should have no passion and romance? What *is* he saying?

3. Share together how you feel about the last paragraph of the devotional, especially this passage: "If a husband loves his wife as he should, she will feel honored and respected. If a wife respects her husband as she should, he will feel loved and appreciated. It's a win-win." The word *if* is tiny, but so important. Talk about how you can change the *if* to *when* in regard to showing each other love and respect.

4. Use the Action item idea to discuss the power of respect. Which is needed more? Love or respect? Can you genuinely have one without the other?

CHAPTER 51: PLUG INTO THE POWER OF OPTIMISM

1. How optimistic are you about your marriage—your commitment as husband and wife to live with love and respect as you glorify Christ? Which phrases best describe you?

    _____ We are struggling but hopeful. Things are much better—we can see daylight.
    _____ We are excited. Love & Respect really works!
    _____ We can't wait to see what God will do next!
    _____ Other: _____

2. This devotional quotes two Scripture verses: Philippians 1:6 and Lamentations 3:21–23. Which one might be the Lord's promise for your marriage? Share ideas on how to make one or both of these verses a prominent part of your daily and weekly routine.

3. In Philippians 1:3–6, Paul is thankful for the Philippian believers and their partnership with him in the gospel from the first day until now. Furthermore, he is confident that God will complete the good work He has begun in them until it is finally finished when Jesus returns. Have you ever seen your marriage as a partnership with the Lord in the gospel? Is spreading the gospel an important part of your marriage? How might it become more important as you serve the Lord as a team?

4. Emerson lists three clues about what it means to be optimistic:

    • Have hope in God.
    • Be thankful.
    • Be enthusiastic about what God is doing and will do.

Which of these best describes how you are experiencing optimism? Which one(s) would you like to experience more?

5. Some people lean toward being pessimistic as a way to protect themselves from being disappointed in the face of unmet expectations. Can this kind of pessimism be a self-fulfilling prophecy? Is it worth it to take the risk of being optimistic?

CHAPTER 52: WHEN IT'S ALL BEEN SAID AND DONE

1. Emerson believes that for the Christ follower the thought of dying should include positive images, not just negative ones. He cites Philippians 1:21, the key verse for this final devotional, and asks, "What *did* Paul mean when he said, 'For to me, to live is Christ and to die is gain'?" What do you think Paul meant?

2. Have you ever considered the meaning of the dash between birth and death dates on a grave marker? The dash represents what we do with our lives. What effect should love and respect have on your dash if you hope to hear the Lord say, "Well done, good and faithful servant" (Matthew 25:21 NIV)? (See Matthew 25:14–21.)

3. Emerson writes: "When it's all been said and done, only one thing will matter." How does he describe this "one thing"? How does he link this last devotional to the one that opened this devotional experience for you and your spouse in chapter 1? The Lord does not demand perfection, but what *does* He want?

4. Use the Action item to reflect on what you are building together in your marriage. How are each of you living out your "dash"?

THE THREE CYCLES OF LOVE & RESPECT

The Love & Respect approach to marriage is based on the awareness that any couple is always potentially on one of three cycles: the Crazy Cycle, the Energizing Cycle, or the Rewarded Cycle. None of these cycles is a permanent, static situation. A lot of couples, however, seem to spend a great deal of time on the Crazy Cycle, which is summed up like this:

Without love, she reacts without respect.
Without respect, he reacts without love.

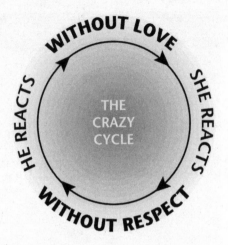

Clearly, the Crazy Cycle triggers and fuels itself. When a wife feels unloved, she tends to react in ways that feel disrespectful to her husband. When a husband feels disrespected, he tends to react in ways that feel unloving to his wife. And around and around they go—on the Crazy Cycle.

The secret to building a happy relationship is to recognize when you are on the Crazy Cycle—when you are not communicating; when you are in some level of conflict, be it mild or severe; or when life together just isn't going well. The Crazy Cycle can be low-key, with both of you trying to keep the lid on, or it can be intense, with angry remarks, biting sarcasm, and worse. The point is that whatever the intensity level of your Crazy Cycle, one and often both of you are doing crazy, dumb things that drive the other one nuts.

EPHESIANS 5:33: THE ANSWER
TO THE CRAZY CYCLE

Scripture offers the answer to the Crazy Cycle in Ephesians 5:33: "Each one of you also must love his wife as he loves himself, and the wife must respect her husband" (NIV). This verse is the summary statement of the greatest treatise on marriage in the New Testament: Ephesians 5:22-33. In verse 33 Paul pens that God commands (not suggests) that husbands *must* love their wives and that wives *must* respect their husbands. What is more, their love and respect must be *unconditional*.

One of my major goals in my writing and speaking is to help husbands and wives grasp the real meaning of that word, *unconditional*. If a wife is lovable, it is easy for her husband to love her, but God's command to love one's wife has nothing to do with her being lovable. And if a husband is respectable, it is easy for his wife to respect him, but God's command to respect one's husband has nothing to do with him being respectable. The Love & Respect message is not about a husband earning his wife's respect by being more loving any more than it is about a wife earning a husband's love by being more respectful. Always, love or respect is given *unconditionally*, according to God's command.

The Love & Respect Connection is stopping the Crazy Cycle in thousands of marriages all over the country and beyond. If husband and wife can commit to meeting each other's primary need—unconditional love for her and unconditional respect for him—they will take a giant step toward keeping the Crazy Cycle under control.

THE ENGERGIZING CYCLE KEEPS THE CRAZY CYCLE IN ITS CAGE

While there are ways to slow or stop the Crazy Cycle (you never get completely off), it can always start up again and usually does, even for happy, well-adjusted couples. The way to keep the

Crazy Cycle in its cage is to get on the Energizing Cycle, which is summed up like this:

His love motivates her respect.
Her respect motivates his love.

Couples are on the Energizing Cycle when they are practicing Love & Respect principles.

C-O-U-P-L-E: Six Ways to Spell Love to Your Wife
To show their love, husbands live out the biblically based principles summed up in the acronym C-O-U-P-L-E.

C: Closeness. She wants you to be close—and not just when you want sex.
O: Openness. She wants you to open up to her, to talk and not be closed off, being angry or disinterested.
U: Understanding. Don't try to "fix" her; just listen—and be considerate when she is upset.

P: Peacemaking. There is incredible power in saying, "Honey, I'm really sorry."

L: Loyalty. Always assure her of your love and commitment.

E: Esteem. Honor your wife; cherish her and treasure her— forever.

If a husband applies just one C-O-U-P-L-E concept each day, he takes giant steps toward making his wife feel unconditionally loved.

C-H-A-I-R-S: Six Ways to Spell Respect to Your Husband
To show their respect, wives live out the principles summed up in the acronym C-H-A-I-R-S.

C: Conquest. Appreciate and thank him for his desire to conquer in his field of work.

H: Hierarchy. Appreciate and thank him for his motivation to protect and provide for you.

A: Authority. Appreciate and thank him for his desire to lead—and don't subvert his leadership.

I: Insight. Appreciate and thank him for his desire to give ideas and advice.

R: Relationship. Appreciate and thank him for his desire that you be his friend and stand shoulder to shoulder with him.

S: Sexuality. Appreciate and respond to his need for you sexually; don't deprive him.

If a wife applies just one C-H-A-I-R-S concept each day, she takes giant steps toward making her husband feel unconditionally respected.

The two acronyms listed above are not just magic words or cure-all formulas. The Energizing Cycle will work only if you do. And as you practice C-O-U-P-L-E or C-H-A-I-R-S, your marriage will be happier, stronger, more biblical, and more honoring to God (see chapters 7 and 8).

THE REWARDED CYCLE: REACHING YOUR ULTIMATE GOAL

Knowing how to stop or slow the Crazy Cycle is good. Practicing the Energizing Cycle with C-O-U-P-L-E and C-H-A-I-R-S is better, but there is another cycle that is all-important for every couple—the Rewarded Cycle, which is summed up like this:

His love blesses regardless of her respect.
Her respect blesses regardless of his love.

The Rewarded Cycle means that God blesses a husband who loves his wife regardless of her level of respect for him, and God blesses a wife who respects her husband regardless of his level of love for her. These blessings are the rewards God gives to those who love or respect a mate because of their own love and reverence for Christ. Christ is the motivation for such action.

When spouses come to me saying the Love & Respect Connection just isn't working, my advice is always the same: Don't give up. Keep doing your part because, in God's economy, no effort to obey Him is wasted. God intends to reward you even if your spouse is unresponsive.

When you love or respect unconditionally, regardless of the outcome, you are following God and His will for you. This is the Rewarded Cycle. You aren't primarily loving your wife or respecting your husband because of what it can do to improve your marriage. Yes, that may be a wonderful by-product, but your real purpose is to love and reverence God by trusting and obeying His commands to you.

In fact, the Rewarded Cycle is as relevant to good marriages as it is to poor ones that seem stuck on the Crazy Cycle. In the long run, husbands and wives should be practicing Love & Respect principles first and foremost out of obedience to God and His command in Ephesians 5:33. This is what *The Love and Respect Devotional* is all about!

≈

Note: The three cycles we have briefly discussed are developed in full detail in *Love & Respect* (Nashville, TN: Integrity Publishers, 2004). Or you can read a condensed one-chapter version in *The Language of Love & Respect* (Nashville, TN: Thomas Nelson, 2007).

DEVOTIONS FOR MARRIED COUPLES: COMMAND OR OPTION?

To even suggest in a devotional for couples that they are under no biblical obligation to have devotions and pray together almost sounds counterproductive. Why, then, this book? Two reasons:

1. I sincerely want to help couples seek God together in prayer and hear from Him in His Word, especially as it relates to love and respect in their marriage.
2. At the same time, I want to help couples who have had difficulty developing any kind of devotional life together. I want to free them from any legalistic impression they may have gotten over the years that all good Christian couples read Scripture and pray together, and if you don't, you are in rebellion against (or at least in neglect of) God's clear command.

If you have been on any kind of guilt trip like this, please stop and get off—now. Scripture holds no specific, mandated command for couples to read the Bible and pray together. There are direct instructions for *individuals* to read Scripture and pray, most familiar of which is Matthew 6:6: "But you, when you pray, go into your inner room, close your door and pray to your Father who is in secret, and your Father who sees what is done in secret will reward you."[1]

Matthew 6:6 is one of a number of places where there are directions to individual believers to speak to God in private prayer. Individual private prayer is not optional and is observed in the life of Jesus and His followers (see Matthew 14:23, 26:36; Acts 10:9, 10:30). What *is* optional is for couples to have devotions together *but only out of free choice*. This is an area of grace. God gives a couple the freedom to decide these things for themselves. Grace means that God does not intend for us to worship, serve, and draw closer to Him grudgingly or under compulsion. See, for example, these passages:

- 2 Corinthians 9:7: "Each one must do just as he has purposed in his heart, not grudgingly or under compulsion, for God loves a cheerful giver."
- Philemon 1:14: "But without your consent I did not want to do anything, so that your goodness would not be, in effect, by compulsion but of your own free will."

So let me state it again to be perfectly clear: I am *not* saying that a couple should not have devotions together. Actually, I encourage this with all my heart—that's why I wrote this book! I *am* saying that having devotions is up to each couple based on their circumstances and how they believe the Lord is directing them. That's my understanding of why the Bible is silent on the subject of devotions for married couples.

The Lord knew that schedules and callings would arise that make it tough for some couples to add joint devotions to their private devotions. For example, I think of the first-century evangelist who traveled away from home and could not pray with his wife on a daily basis. God allows couples the freedom and flexibility to enter into marital prayer if they can, but circumstances and service may dictate otherwise.

You may still be wondering how I can be so sure Scripture does not command that husbands and wives have devotions together, preferably on a daily basis. For years in the pastorate I taught couples exactly that, but the more I studied the Word to get actual confirmation of this seemingly cozy and comfortable concept, the less I could find. Eventually, I had to face squarely what Scripture and church history really had to say.

Here is what I have found. In the first century couples did not have copies of the Scriptures. The early believers did not have the parchments upon which the sacred texts were etched. They could only hear the public readings. For instance, in the synagogue they would listen to Moses, read from a particular parchment (Acts 13:27; 2 Corinthians 3:15), or in the churches they'd gather to hear the reading of Paul's letters to the churches (Colossians 4:16; 1 Thessalonians 5:27; 1 Timothy 4:13). And in these corporate settings individuals were expected to "let the word of Christ richly dwell within" them (Colossians 3:16) and, as Paul exhorts in Ephesians 5:19, "speak to one another with psalms, hymns and spiritual songs" (NIV).

Note that following Ephesians 5:19, Paul moves on to speak specifically of marriage (Ephesians 5:22–33). As you are well aware, there are many rich truths in this passage in regard to marriage, Christ and His church, and love and respect. Based on these understandings of marriage, it is not hard to picture a scene where husband and wife, returning home from a gathering of believers for worship, would share with each other what they had learned that day in church where the Word of God had been preached. But there is no specific command in Ephesians 5:22–33 to have devotions together.

As for praying together, we do not find any specific instructions to husbands and wives to pray together as couples during daily devotions. The silence on this strikes me as odd since one would think that Paul would have put much stronger emphasis on telling couples to pray together than on advising them in such matters as having sex (see, for example, 1 Corinthians 7:1–4). But what about 1 Corinthians 7:5–6? "Stop depriving one another, except by agreement for a time, so that you may devote yourselves to prayer, and come together again so that Satan will not tempt you because of your lack of self-control. But this I say by way of concession, not of command." For years I taught that this passage meant that couples were to pray together while abstaining from sex. However, upon deeper reflection, I realized that Paul could have been recommending that they separate for the purpose of prayer, but not stay away from each other too long lest Satan tempt them sexually due to their lack of self-control. Perhaps Paul could have meant that couples pray together, but not have sex together, but there is no way to be dogmatic on what he was trying to say. I had to back off on how I had once applied this text to couples. I could not use it to say, "Thus saith the Lord: pray together as a husband and wife during your daily devotions together."[2]

What about 1 Peter 3:7? Paul instructs husbands to live with their wives in an understanding way so that their prayers will not be hindered. The primary interpretation of many commentators sees Peter referring to the prayers of the husband being hindered, but some scholars see the passage referring to a couple struggling in their marriage and finding their prayers as a couple hindered. At one time, I chose to use this second option and encouraged couples to keep their relationship up to date in order for them to pray together. But the more I studied and taught on I Peter 3:7, the more I saw that there was no way to be sure I could use it to declare with unction, "Thus saith the Lord: keep your marriage great in order to pray together." I believe this is true, but I could not announce that based on this text. I started to teach what I teach today: that the passage refers to the husband's private prayer life. Peter is telling the husband to treasure his wife and treat her with esteem as part of keeping his prayer life effective before God.

Having said all this, I must hasten to add that the Bible more than implies that a couple can and should pray together at certain times. For example, in Scripture we see believers gathering with other believers to pray (Acts 1:14; 2:1, 42, 46; 4:24-31; 6:4). Surely in these settings there were husbands and wives praying together along with other believers.

Note, too, that there need not be a large group of one hundred or more or a smaller group of a dozen or so. Jesus teaches that it takes just two people to agree together and He will act: "For where two or three have gathered together in My name, I am there in their midst" (Matthew 18:20). I realize that the context of this well-known passage concerns instructions on invoking church discipline, but I believe that Jesus is also teaching the church a principle about praying together in His name. Every husband and wife can be encouraged to act on this principle, knowing that two praying people—just two—can make a huge difference in God's kingdom.

Another good example is Ephesians 6:18: "With all prayer and petition pray at all times in the Spirit, and with this in view, be on the alert with all perseverance and petition for all the saints." Surely believing husbands and wives were included in Paul's frame of reference here, particularly since he had just given to the church his final words on marriage a few paragraphs earlier in Ephesians 5:22–33. In Ephesians 6:18, Paul could be urging private individual prayer or corporate prayer, but I don't think Paul is saying, "This does not apply to spouses. Don't you husbands and wives pray together for the saints. Keep it private, or keep it corporate but absolutely no marital prayer about this!"

I am sure you detect that I am using a sarcastic tone here to make the point that God wants couples to pray together for various reasons. But my original point remains the same: *there is no direct command in Scripture to couples to pray together for devotional purposes.* Where then does this leave us? I believe we are free to make an informed choice based on what seems best at this season of our marriage. If you and your spouse find it an opportune time to make a concerted effort to read Scripture and pray together, I invite you to join Sarah and me in doing these fifty-two devotionals together. And we all do this not because we have to, but because we want to seek God as couples on some kind of regular basis during a certain period of our lives.

Exactly how a "regular basis" might look to you is your decision. You may have already seen our suggested one-chapter-a-week scenario in "Options for Using This Book on Your Own Terms" (page xvii). But this is only a suggestion. You can adapt it, change it, or ignore it completely. As I said, my goal is to help you work out a way to have devotions on some basis, according to what God appears to be telling you. Perhaps this will mean using chapters in this book individually for a while and doing little or nothing together. But then there may be times when you want to share what you have learned and perhaps pray together. Every couple is at a different point on the continuum—from couples who have no problem having devotions together and do it with comfort and much benefit, to couples who struggle to one degree or another, to those who have schedules and callings that do not permit this right now.

And there is also the couple in which one spouse wants to do devotions, but the other flatly refuses. My advice to the one who wants to have devotions is to relax. You cannot and must not force another person to pray with you and discuss a biblical passage with you. Do these devotionals on your own. Obey Jesus' teaching to pray in your closet to Abba Father. Meditate on what God reveals, live out as best you can your part of the Love & Respect Connection, and let Him do the rest.

One more thing: Sarah and I would love to hear from you. When God speaks to you from one of the devotionals, either as a couple or individually, tell us what He has revealed. Write us at devotionals@loveandrespect.com and we will post your thoughts. Together we can inspire and encourage one another!

WHERE TO GET HELP FOR SEXUAL OR FINANCIAL PROBLEMS

The organizations listed are trustworthy sources of Godly-wise assistance to couples with continuing issues or questions regarding sex or finances. These organizations may be able to refer you to advisors or therapists in your local area with whom they cooperate, or they can advise you online or over the phone. Also, keep in mind that your pastor or local church may have recommendations concerning resources related to finances or sexual adjustment.

FOR HELP REGARDING SEXUAL QUESTIONS OR ISSUES:

www.pureintimacy.org (Focus on the Family)

FOR HELP REGARDING MANAGEMENT OF FINANCES:

www.daveramsey.com (Financial Peace)
www.crown.org (Crown Financial Ministries)

NOTES

CHAPTER 13: THOSE WHO PRAY TOGETHER LEARN TO LOVE & RESPECT TOGETHER

1. While the yes-no-or-wait scenario is true, atheists and skeptics can always say, "Well, one of these three will always happen due to the law of probability, so this proves nothing more than that flipping a coin shows heads 50 percent of the time." My answer to that: You make a reasonable charge. However, the one who chooses to follow Christ makes a decision to trust the resurrected and ascended Lord at His invitation. One prays because one believes Jesus Christ is alive and is listening, even if the answer appears to be no. In Matthew 7:7, Jesus said, "Ask, and it will be given to you; seek, and you will find; knock, and it will be opened to you." He went on to say something most wonderful in 7:9-11: "Or what man is there among you who, when his son asks for a loaf, will give him a stone? Or if he asks for a fish, he will not give him a snake, will he? If you then, being evil, know how to give good gifts to your children, how much more will your Father who is in heaven give what is good to those who ask Him!" In short, Jesus would ignore the question of probability and instruct us to trust the Father's goodness to respond to our asking, according to His perfect, sovereign will. For Sarah and me, it isn't a matter of "rolling the dice," but simply of trusting God as our Father—and Father knows best.

CHAPTER 15: TO TELL THE TRUTH . . . IS NOT ALWAYS EASY

1. When Paul says we are to tell our neighbors the truth, he is adding holy emphasis from the Old Testament by quoting Zechariah 8:16. A

prophet to Jews who had returned from exile in Babylon to rebuild the temple, Zechariah spelled out how they could know God's blessing: "These are things which you should do: speak the truth to one another; judge with truth and judgment for peace in your gates." From the Old Testament to the New, God places a premium on telling the truth, the whole truth, and nothing but the truth.

CHAPTER 16: FEELINGS AREN'T FACTS—ALWAYS SORT IT OUT

1. James Strong, S.T.D., LL.D., Hebrew and Greek Dictionaries taken from *Strong's Exhaustive Concordance* (1890), Sword of the Lord software, H4194: death (natural or violent); concretely the *dead*, their place or state (hades); figuratively *pestilence, ruin*.

CHAPTER 18: JOHN WOODEN: A LOVE & RESPECT LEGACY FOR THE AGES

1. Steve Jamison, "The Joy of the Journey," The Journey, The Official Site of Coach John Wooden, www.coachwooden.com/index2.html (accessed 5 June 11).
2. "Woodenisms," Bill Walton.com, www.billwalton.com/woodenisms (accessed 5 June 11).
3. Greg Asimakoupoulos, "Remembering a Life Well Lived," The Amy Foundation, http://www.amyfound.org/index.html.
4. Ibid.
5. Ibid.
6. "Woodenisms," Bill Walton.com, www.billwalton.com/woodenisms (accessed 5 June 11).
7. Asimakoupoulos, "Remembering a Life Well Lived."

CHAPTER 35: IT *IS* ALL ABOUT ME, AFTER ALL

1. Postmodernism is closely associated with New Age thinking, which believes we find "God" within ourselves, that there is no Creator

who provides salvation. See Jim Leffel and Dennis McCallum, "The Postmodern Impact: Religion," chap. 12 in *The Death of Truth*, ed. Dennis McCallum (Minneapolis: Bethany House Publishers, 1996).
2. Referenced by Charles Colson, "Marriage as Therapy or Covenant?" *BreakPoint*, June 11, 2010.

CHAPTER 37: TO OVERCOME THE PAST, FOCUS ON THE PRIZE

1. "New York Giants Head Coach: Tom Coughlin," NFL.com, www .nfl.com/teams/coaches?coaType=head&team=NYG (accessed 6 June 11).

CHAPTER 45: HOW POSITIVE ARE YOU WITH EACH OTHER?

1. For the full context of Philippians 4:8–9, go back to verses 6–7. Paul instructs us to take everything to God, who will give us peace that transcends all understanding. With this kind of peace and assurance, we can think as He directs in verses 8–9.
2. This story, used with permission, was shared with the author by Norm and Bobbe Evans, leaders of Pro Athletes Outreach, which was organized more than forty years ago to evangelize and disciple professional football and baseball players. Norm (president), Bobbe (executive director), and their staff seek to help pros, coaches, and their families to maximize their platforms of influence, effectively communicate their faith in God through Jesus Christ, and strengthen their personal relationships, marriages, parenting, finances, and faith.

CHAPTER 46: DO YOU EVER PLAY THE BLAME GAME?

1. Quote shared personally with author and used with permission by Barb Whitehead, who played on the LPGA tour from 1984 to 2002. She qualified for the tour on her second try, after competing for the University of Tulsa and Iowa State, where she was an All-American her freshman year. She was known on tour by her maiden name, Barb Thomas, until 1996, when she married Trent Whitehead, who

later caddied for her from 2000 to 2002. In 1995 she recorded her only tour victory, the Cup of Noodles Hawaiian Open, where she shot a career-low round of 66. Barb recorded five holes-in-one during tour competition, including two in 1998. The Whiteheads have two daughters, Sarah Ellen, born in 1999, and Emma Grace, born in 2001.

CHAPTER 52: WHEN IT'S ALL BEEN SAID AND DONE

1. This personal benediction on all who seek to practice love and respect in their marriage is based on Hebrews 13:21–22, with paraphrasing by the author and from Eugene Peterson's *The Message*.

APPENDIX A: DISCUSSION QUESTIONS

1. "Woodenisms," Bill Walton.com, www.billwalton.com/woodenisms (accessed 5 June 11).

APPENDIX C: DEVOTIONS FOR MARRIED COUPLES: COMMAND OR OPTION?

1. For Jesus' entire teaching on prayer in this scene in Matthew 6, see verses 5–13. It is interesting that in verses 5 and 7 the Greek pronoun translated as "you" is in the plural. Only in verse 6 is the Greek word for "you" in the singular, in order to stress private prayer to God. Note also that Jesus goes on to teach his disciples what is commonly known as the Lord's Prayer, in which all the pronouns are in the plural due to the corporate nature of the prayer. A married couple can repeat the Lord's Prayer together if they so choose, but the passage is not commanding them to have devotions together.
2. All this is not to say that Scripture does not record instances where spouses prayed for one another. See, for example, Isaac praying on behalf of Rebekah and her barrenness (Genesis 25:21), and an angel of the Lord referring to Zacharias's prayers for Elizabeth because she could have no children due to their advanced ages (Luke 1:5–14).

ABOUT THE AUTHOR

D
r. Emerson Eggerichs is an internationally known expert on male-female relationships. The author of several books, including the national bestseller *Love & Respect*, which has sold more than 1.3 million copies, Emerson and his wife, Sarah, present Love & Respect Conferences both live and by video to more than 50,000 people each year, including sessions with the NFL, PGA, and members of congress.

Prior to launching their ministry, Dr. Eggerichs was the senior pastor of Trinity Church in Lansing, Michigan, for nineteen years. He has graduate degrees from Wheaton College and Dubuque Seminary and a PhD from Michigan State University.

Married since 1973, Emerson and Sarah live in Grand Rapids, Michigan, and have three adult children. He is the founder and president of Love and Respect Ministries.